The In

to

Healthy Workplace Culture

Prevent Toxic Work Environments,

Bullying, Sexual Harassment, and

Discrimination

Meredith Holley

Copyright

in order to create a healthy environment. The practical steps in this book are a roadmap to creating an environment that allows people to thrive. It is our responsibility to make these changes now so it doesn't fall on the next generation."

— Mandy Vickers
RN, Certified Life Coach, Founder of Raise Your Girls Coaching.

"While this book is aimed at business owners, every manager should invest in understanding this space. As a manager in the tech industry, I see the issues Meredith walks through happen often. The first time I dealt with an employee bullying situation it was overwhelming. Often we aren't prepared. This is your opportunity to better prepare yourself and your team to handle conflicts."

— Meg Weber
Executive Producer, Director of Creative Operations

"As one of two women on my team, I'm often faced with untrue and offensive gender stereotypes, and question how best to respond. I want to advocate for myself, work to change perception where possible, and help improve things for other women, without alienating or offending my cisgender, straight, white male coworkers. Meredith's advice in The Inclusive Leader's Guide to Healthy Workplace Culture has helped me accomplish these goals while maintaining an open, cooperative, and respectful team dynamic. I have appreciated the changes I've seen on my team, and in myself, as I've worked to apply her ideas."

— Erica Smith
Workforce Management Reporting Analyst, E*Trade

"As a Marine Corps Judge Advocate, I have successfully defended Marines accused of sexual assault by other Marines. Similarly, as a Company Commander, I was part of the official process to investigate and adjudicate various claims of harassment, discrimination, and sexual assault. I saw firsthand, from both vantage points, how devastating it can be for people on both sides of an accusation to take time out of their careers to go through the investigation and adjudication process. I am also a Gracie Jiu Jitsu instructor where I teach men, women, and children to defend themselves in situations where they may feel powerless. From these experiences, I have learned that the more we empower people to encounter dangerous behavior effectively, the better they can protect themselves and prevent a crisis. Feelings of powerlessness and an imbalance of power exist in most businesses, especially when it comes to harassment and discrimination. Unfortunately, dealing with them through the investigation and adjudication process can derail a company and leave all parties feeling like they have lost. In her insightful book, Meredith expertly explains how to take the appropriate proactive steps to correct this imbalance before it becomes a crisis, and also how to deal with crises effectively when they happen. I stress to clients all the time how important it is to define what you want your culture to be and then to actively work to cultivate and keep it. This book shows you how to do just that. If you are a leader who wants to get the best out of your people and ensure that your company is a place where your people feel respected, valued, and supported, then you need to listen closely to what she has to say!"

— Robert Heath, Sr.
Marine Corps Veteran, CEO of Legacy Leadership Consulting, Founder of the Legacy Empowerment Academy, and bestselling author of Why Can't People Just Do Their Jobs? The Empowering Leader's Guide to More Fulfillment, Less Stress, and Getting the Best out of your Team

Dedication

For every business owner, boss lady, and scaling entrepreneur, who is bringing good into the world and changing it for the better. This book is to help in times when the work family gets challenging.

Table of Contents

Introduction: The Problem of Toxic Workplace Culture

When I listened to Rhea's voicemail message, I could hear the panic in her voice. She said that she had made an appointment for later that week, but she felt she needed to talk to someone right away because she was so concerned about the situation that she and the other owners of her company were facing. I called her back and she explained to me that a man who worked for her had accused a female co-worker of sexual assault and harassment. She wanted to make sure everyone was safe and that she was conducting an appropriate investigation, and she was also worried that these allegations could ruin her business's reputation in the community.

Rhea explained to me that she has a background in teaching sex-positive classes, and she believes strongly that shame around sexual experiences is unhealthy. She also had her own experience of sexual assault that was traumatizing, and she understood what it felt like to be victimized. The employee accused of harassment vehemently denied that anything non-consensual had occurred between the two employees, and Rhea didn't know who to believe. She wanted to protect her employees, and she also believed in the work her company was doing and wanted to protect that. She didn't want to think of her business's health being threatened by a cultural problem with her employees. She and a few co-workers had intentionally left another company to start this business because she saw that employees in her field were not treated well. She felt she was doing everything for her employees, even sometimes sacrificing her own salary, and so hearing allegations of abuse felt devastating.

Rhea's male employee who was alleging the abuse believed he was being treated differently as a man than a woman alleging abuse would have been. He thought that a man accused of sexual harassment would have been fired immediately, and that it was unfair for a woman accused of harassment to be heard and able to stay in her job for a day longer. Rhea put the female employee on leave, but honestly Rhea did not see things the way her male employee did. She felt that men are often given a great deal of leeway when they are accused of harassment, but she felt conflicted about whether that meant she should continue the tradition of giving leeway to someone accused of harassment or whether she should take a harsher stance to honor victims of harassment. To top it off, all of this was happening while Brett Kavanaugh was being confirmed to the Supreme Court. The tensions were high, both about the issue of whether victims should be believed and whether perpetrators should be given a second chance and considered "innocent until proven guilty."

Rhea's business had grown up from a small group of friends to thirty-five to forty employees. She did not have the opportunity to interact with each of the employees all of the time, and so it was a shock to her to find out that anyone could feel unsafe in the workspace she had taken so much care to create. She loved each of her employees, and hugging was a regular greeting in the workplace. Would this mean that she and her employees should be afraid of hugging each other as a greeting because someone might take it the wrong way?

Rhea said that this allegation was so stressful to her that she had trouble sleeping in the days leading up to our meeting. She felt high anxiety and nauseated at the idea of what could happen to her employees and her business. Others told her she should not be so concerned. Of the small handful of people who heard about these allegations, some told Rhea they were confident that the relationship the two employees had was consensual and that the male employee was using the Kavanaugh hearings as social leverage for himself. Rhea believed it was not that simple. She remembered her own experience and knew what it felt like to be disbelieved and not know what to do. She had done tremendous personal work to be able to lead the business she was leading, and she knew how painful it was to view herself as a victim of a sexual crime.

When we met, I mentioned to Rhea what I often see when I am working with employees as a lawyer and life coach in high-conflict harassment and discrimination situations. I let her know that often when there are allegations of sexual harassment, the accusing employee views themselves as having a powerless role and engages in people-pleasing behavior. So, even if the accused employee did not mean to harass the accusing employee, the accusing employee may still have had an experience of victimization. To say it more simply, one person might not like something another is doing, but might feel powerless to say no. The second person genuinely doesn't know they're doing something unwanted, but the first person still experiences trauma. Rhea immediately looked at me and said, "That's it! I think that is exactly what is going on here." She showed me the investigation she and the other owners had done, and it supported two very different viewpoints. In the investigation notes it was clear that the accusing employee himself recognized that in the moment he had not told the woman he believed was harassing him that her behavior was unwanted. The woman said she believed that the man actively consented to and liked her behavior; the man said he believed he was not allowed to say no.

It is one thing to understand the power imbalance between two people, but it is a separate thing to help both people see their own power and resolve a high-conflict issue. When I started working with Rhea's employees, both were in complete crisis. Both had spoken with the police and had fears about a criminal investigation. Both spent over an hour crying and/or yelling to initiate our conversations, and I sat with both of them for four hours for our initial meeting to really absorb their perspectives on their stories and offer them the basics of what I teach. The next time we met, both were still angry and hurt. Before our third conversation, though, both had apologized to each other for their part in what they agreed was a complicated relationship. They agreed that they wanted to try to work together professionally. Rhea was able to implement rules that would make the workplace safer, with specific expectations around physical contact and respect.

One of Rhea's business partners expressed that she had been really worried that their work family would have to become a cold place after these allegations of harassment, with no hugging, joking, or personal relationships allowed. But, after these employees did the hard work to shift the power dynamics in their situation and own responsibility for their own thoughts, feelings, and actions, she noticed positive attitude changes and more engagement from them.

Workplace cultural health problems don't start out as crisis conflict, but they can easily become that when they are ignored. I have seen businesses shut down after harassment allegations, and I have also seen businesses and their employees thrive and grow around these conflicts. Ignoring and covering up harassment and discrimination does not solve it, it just feeds the toxicity and gives it room to grow. Once it is big enough, it can swallow entire organizations. Resolving a cultural health conflict never means covering it up or pretending abusive behavior is okay. But, when employers can take an active role in diagnosing their company's cultural health and effectively resolving conflict issues by understanding and teaching how power dynamics impact the workplace, it is possible for harassment and discrimination allegations to ignite growth in the business, rather than destruction. I hope to share in this book the process I help businesses go through to resolve crisis conflict and create healthy workplace cultures.

Chapter 1: Pulling the "Push Only" Door

"The only other advice I have is that things are really sexist, and we just have to deal with it."

Early in my legal career, this was what I heard when I approached another employment attorney about sexual harassment I was experiencing. At the time, I was trying to take preventative steps before the harassment got too bad because I loved the work I was doing. I asked this lawyer how to set clear boundaries in my job with a much older man who seemed interested in me. I was so discouraged by the advice to "just deal with it" that I stopped talking about my experience as it got worse and worse over the course of a year.

Every time my boss would rub my shoulders or lean his body against mine, I would experience a complete freeze and dissociation. I found myself unable to say anything, even though I had never been someone to back down from defending myself. I had experienced harassment in the past and had always been able to stop it and stand up for myself. I knew I was smart and tough, but somehow this was different than what I had experienced in the past. I was constantly holding my breath and felt afraid all the time.

One of the reasons this experience was different was that I was in my dream job. I was representing women in sexual harassment lawsuits... while I was being sexually harassed myself. I was saying to women on the phone what I had been instructed to say ("Call us back if you get fired, but otherwise there's not much the law can do to protect you while you're still working"), and at the same time, I was experiencing the ramifications of that kind of advice myself. In law firms that represent employees, the advice to "call us back if you get fired" is often spoken over and over again, no matter how painful it is for the attorney or the employee. This is because the law only addresses harassment and discrimination under narrow circumstances and firing an employee for a discriminatory reason tends to be the simplest to identify. When lawyers file lawsuits in other situations they can be expensive for clients and have no guaranteed win. In these situations, lawyers are turning employees away in many senses to protect them rather than giving them false expectations, but that doesn't make it easier.

I know how this feels on both sides: Terrible. When someone seeks you out as a resource of support in a vulnerable position, it feels terrible to turn them away. When you seek someone out as a resource and they don't know how to help, your situation can feel hopeless and lonely. Even though I considered myself a feminist and didn't want to blame myself for the harassment I was experiencing, I changed the clothes I wore, tried to speak differently, and withdrew. When I was experiencing harassment, I would guess that about eighty percent of my brain was taken up trying to guess whether I was safe in a situation and figure out how to keep myself safe without losing my job the next time I was around my harasser.

When I felt like I had no choice but to turn away other employees in the same situation, I felt even more hopeless. I thought putting up with harassment couldn't be the only way for women to advance in their careers, but the only other options seemed to be that some women were inherently lucky enough to never face harassment or other women knew something I didn't know. Since I apparently wasn't inherently lucky, the thought that there was a solution somewhere seemed like the only possibility with any hope. It was a slim hope, and the answers I was getting were not encouraging, but it was a strong enough hope to keep me going.

I saw this same experience in many other clients I was serving – from employees facing race discrimination or retaliation for making a workers' compensation claim to people trying to navigate the insurance and medical systems after a car crash. I could get a successful legal result for them, but I didn't have the answer for them about how to really recover from their trauma, and some of them appeared to be without hope. They heard the same kind of things I heard when talking to friends: "I don't take things like that so seriously, but I'm pretty resilient," "It's probably not as bad as you think, and if you stick it out it will get better," "You could try to file a lawsuit, but you'll probably have to quit your job," or "I'm pretty tough when it comes to things like that, so I just make a joke and brush it off."

I had been firmly told that making my harasser happy was my one priority in order to keep my job. But it appeared that allowing him to lean his full body against mine to read over my shoulder, rub his hands up and down my arms and shoulders, comment on my appearance and clothing, and criticize my every move was what it would take to make him happy. I felt stuck, and after I reported him to my supervisors twice, I thought maybe there was no answer to what I was going through. But I also believed at the time that I could be in physical danger. I often worked at night and was alone in the office, and like most women, I was raised to believe that being at work after dark was dangerous. I thought maybe my only option was to quit. I thought that quitting meant I would have to move away because my harasser was such a prominent person in my community. I thought I would not be able to continue to work unless I had his support.

I remember walking to work, listening to podcasts, and also listening to my heart pound in fear. I felt the physical tension of anxiety and fear almost constantly. It seemed unthinkable to leave my job, though. Not only would it be giving up on a career I had worked so hard for, but also it would be abandoning clients I loved. It seemed like there was no solution. The only two options I was presented with were to quit and sue or to accept the behavior. It did not seem like those could be the only two options, but I just could not find any others.

That was until a series of events brought me to the tools I teach in this book. It's funny to me to write a book like this or to have written my previous self-help book Career Defense 101: How to Stop Sexual Harassment Without Quitting Your Job. It's funny because I've always been skeptical of self-help books, and I hated the idea that "positive-thinking" leads to people magically getting rewards from the universe. This always seemed to me like a way to blame people for flaws in the system that they had no control over. I have always believed that "magic cures" are a way for con artists to manipulate people looking for an easy answer.

So, I'm a little embarrassed to tell you that for me, the tools I learned that turned my harassment situation around absolutely felt like a magic cure to me. I teach those tools more specifically in Career Defense 101, as they relate to employees who want to make a difference in their workplace. It was like someone handed me the keys to a door that all these people had access to, but I had never even seen. Or, it was like I was trying to find my phone in a dark room, having an impossible time, and then someone flipped a light switch. It was a really outrageously hard magic cure, despite its simplicity. But just the fact that there was any cure was enough for me, when I had previously thought there might be no good solution. It was like I was pulling a "push only" door for a year, and then someone walked up and showed me how to push the door open. Basically it was a simple shift that meant everything.

So, if you are skeptical that a solution to employee conflict exists, I get it. I was there too, but as an unhappy, afraid, distracted employee, who also cared about and wanted to keep her job and did not want to file a lawsuit. At the same time, I was supervising and managing others, and serving clients. I had concerns about how they were treated and my obligations to them as well. The thing I have found out since learning these tools is that some people just intuitively understand these tools and see life in this way. Many, many of us do not, though. So, even though these tools seem natural to me now, after having practiced them for years, I still encounter people every day who are learning them for the first time. The way these tools will apply to you and your business will be unique, and so if this seems challenging, it is totally normal to need support from a lawyer or power dynamics facilitator.

Many employees who encounter harassment or discrimination do not have the training or background I had at the point at which I encountered harassment that stopped me dead in my tracks. I thought what I knew about negotiation and legal rights alone should have taught me how to handle any situation, but they did not. What I teach in this book is the best I know of what actually works to resolve high-conflict, high-drama employment situations.

Even though it's hard for many of us to even acknowledge, the emotional and physical impacts of harassment and discrimination are not the only issues many business owners need to face when they have employees. When we love our employees and think of our workplace as a family, it is stressful to think about anyone in that work family feeling unsafe or anyone in that work family creating an unsafe situation.

On top of that, though, allegations of harassment and discrimination can seriously impact how the public sees a business. A Harvard Business Review Study published in June 2018, titled How Sexual Harassment Affects a Company's Public Image, reported that a single allegation of sexual harassment can create the public impression that an entire organization has a systemic cultural problem. The study also reported that if the public hears an organization's response was timely, informative, and considerate to the victim, it eliminates the public perception that the organization has a systemic cultural problem. So, one incident of sexual harassment can significantly hurt a business, unless the business responds effectively to restore the company to a position of cultural health. As you probably know, the #MeToo movement generated interest in sexual harassment, and that promoted research studies and surveys on sexual harassment in 2018, showing how common sexual harassment is. This study is one of those.

As a white woman, sexual harassment is a way I typically experience discrimination, and it is also a particular focus of my business, in part because of my personal understanding of it. So, if I focus some information in this book toward sexual harassment, it is not meant to minimize any other experiences, but in part because it is my personal experience. On top of that, though, the #MeToo focus on sexual harassment has generated very interesting statistics and research focused on harassment that extrapolate to other forms of discrimination as well. For example, not only have we seen CEOs step down because of sexual harassment allegations, we have seen bakeries close down after refusing to provide wedding cakes for gay marriages. There are approximately 3-4,000 more charges filed with the Equal Employment Opportunity Commission for race discrimination than sex discrimination each year, and each of those likely represents this type of crisis situation for a business. Even though this story and others in this book focus on sexual harassment as the example and as my particular expertise, these studies can inform other areas of toxic workplace culture as well.

In my situation, after I learned the tools in this book I was able to encounter the harassment differently. My harasser apologized, stopped touching me, and we worked together safely and respectfully for years after. What was for so long a devastating experience to me became something I look back on as empowering.

When I started using these tools with the employees I was representing in discrimination lawsuits, I saw huge shifts in their abilities to follow through, tell their story clearly, and advocate for themselves and other employees. For example, early on when I learned these tools, I was working with one woman who had been fired from a career she had been in for twenty-six years because she took time off to take a newly-placed foster child to a medical appointment. She had a very sympathetic case for family-leave retaliation, but when I asked her simple questions to prepare her for an investigation interview, she went down long tangential descriptions and blamed herself for things that were clearly not her fault. I was worried her case would not be successful because she could not tell her story clearly. I tested out whether these tools could help her be clear and confident in her answers to an investigator. After working with her through a sample of the process, I saw her give clear, confident, understandable responses to the investigator.

In another situation, I worked with Naomi, who had been experiencing harassment for eight years and was afraid for her life after bringing claims (I talk more about Naomi in Chapter 4). Naomi was already experiencing panic attacks when she came to me and after a few months of pursuing her claims, she became unable to leave her house because she was so afraid. We settled her lawsuit before I learned the tools I teach in this book, and even though it was a great settlement and she expressed appreciation for it, I could tell that on the inside she was still suffering. What use is money from a settlement if you're too afraid to go outside? I thought about her all the time and it felt like my legal skills were in many ways useless if I was limited to offering traumatized employees a lump sum of money. I reached out to Naomi later, letting her know about what I had learned and what I teach in Career Defense 101, and we agreed to work together on those tools. After a few weeks of work, she was not only able to go outside, but she found the motivation to apply for a new job she was excited about. She completely turned her situation around and was able to take control of her life again.

I now teach these tools through a Power Dynamics Master Certification Training, which I offer to employees who come to me either on their own or through their employers. I offer Workplace Cultural Health Facilitations for companies, and I train Power Dynamics Facilitators to work in companies and maintain cultural health. I get the most excited when an employer knows an employee is struggling and reaches out to get that employee help before the employee is even ready to complain about their situation. For example, in one situation an employer saw that her employee made an unusual mistake and knew something bigger was going on. The employer knew that the employee was better than the mistake and so it seemed unlike her, but the employer had also caught wind that another employee was hassling the woman who made the mistake. Once I started to work with the woman it became clear that even though no one else in the office knew about it, the employee had an invisible disability that she was very self-conscious about. What looked like simple "hassling," average "meanness," or even "bullying" on the outside felt like harassment and discrimination to this employee, and she was having an internal breakdown about how to deal with it. It was severely distracting from her ability to do her work. She wanted to quit and give up when we first started working together, but when she could see her situation through a more powerful, compassionate perspective, she was able to see how advocating for her career did not need to look like terrifying confrontation or rebellion. She could better see that she could take steps to keep herself safe in the workplace in a way that felt natural to her, and if she did that, she could still pursue a career she loved.

While lawsuits are unpredictable and expensive, I know when I can get involved early, I can help the employee learn how to stop harassment in the moment so that both the employee and the employer benefit. When an employer comes to me ahead of time, I offer everything I know to the employee to prevent the situation and I take a mediator position related to the employee's situation with the company. This means that if the employee is later unhappy enough to file a lawsuit (which I have not yet seen), I would be conflicted from representing them, and my work with the employee would be confidential to the extent possible under law. The employer has also taken proactive steps to protect her company and prevent discrimination and so on a purely strategic level, this makes a harassment lawsuit much more difficult.

When an employee comes to me on their own to stop a harassing environment, I still use the law in that employee's favor, up to and including filing a lawsuit when necessary. The law is just one way to set a consequence for dangerous behavior. But it is so much more rewarding and powerful to see employees able to bring their full value and their full skills to their jobs, without having to worry about toxic behavior at work.

My vision of the law is that we use it as a problem-solving tool, not as a mechanism for powerful people to abuse the disenfranchised, not as a mechanism of divisiveness. A good job is always better than a good lawsuit. A productive employee is always better than an investigation. When employees are forced to leave jobs, it hurts both the employee and the business owner. Many employees essentially become career refugees, moving from job to job without any safe place to land. It allows harassment to thrive in a business. Often, good, inclusive leaders in a business are not even aware the harassment is happening or truly don't know how to deal with it. They are seeing the harasser with such a different perspective than the harassed employee that it is hard for them to imagine the company's cultural health, and thereby its productivity and ability to serve clients, being at risk. Most business owners and managers want to be focused on their work and their service to their clients, not monitoring the interpersonal interactions of their employees. And they should be focused on serving clients.

Creating systemic processes to maintain cultural health is like having a hygiene routine for your business. It does not need to take all of your focus or tank your productivity. In fact, it should enhance productivity and allow your employees to truly, wholeheartedly engage in their work.

What I want you to know is that if you have experienced toxic workplace culture, or even chronic anxiety at work, either as an employee or as a boss (or both like me!), there is nothing wrong with you. There are solutions. I hope for your sake that you have always been able to push open the doors in your life. But, if you have been pulling on the "push only" doors, I hope the tools I share in this book help you make a shift, like they did with me.

Chapter 2: Three Steps to Cultural Health

You may be thinking, "That could never happen in my company (I hope!)," and I hear you. The public often has the perception that "bad" companies have discrimination and "good" companies do not. We think that "bad" people harass and discriminate, while "good" people naturally know how to be fair and promote equality. This makes it really hard to talk about workplace cultural health issues and shuts down conversations. The reality is that most women, minorities, and people with targeted cultural characteristics have experienced harassment and discrimination. That very fact makes it clear that it's not just "bad" companies or "bad" people who are being harassing or discriminatory.

In 2018, NPR released a survey conducted by Stop Street Harassment that showed that eighty-one percent of women report experiencing sexual harassment. Thirty-eight percent of women report experiencing sexual harassment at work. Only thirty-one percent of women said they felt comfortable reporting harassment at work. This makes sense because the federal Equal Employment Opportunity Commission (EEOC) reports that approximately seventy-five percent of those who report harassment or discrimination experience retaliation. A Marketplace-Edison Research Poll showed that about half of women who experience harassment at work leave their careers. This means that approximately nineteen percent of women (about one in five) leave a career because of sexual harassment.

If thirty-eight percent of women report experiencing sexual harassment at work, it is not possible that all of those women are working at "bad" companies unless we believe that about half of the employers in the United States (the ones employing these women) are just inherently "bad" and these women are all working for the same companies. Then, beyond that, we would have to believe that an even larger percentage of employers who employ people of color are "bad," based on the higher reports of race discrimination. The fact that there are thousands more EEOC charges related to race than sex indicates that people of color face a staggeringly high amount of discrimination and race-based harassment. The statistics themselves show that most, if not all, of our companies need to look at harassment and discrimination as a serious issue in order to be more productive.

The Society of Human Resource Management estimates that it costs an employer about one fifth of an employee's salary to replace that employee. If we only consider these issues as it applies to women, and one in five women leaves a career because of sexual harassment, ignoring the problem is an incredibly expensive investment in the status quo.

Good Businesses Have a Harder Time

One of the factors that made it harder for the employees in Rhea's company, which I talked about in the Introduction, to talk about the problems they were facing before they became a crisis was that they loved their work and were dedicated to the mission of the company, which worked with a very vulnerable population of clients. It might surprise you to hear that owners of "good" businesses have more hurdles to creating a healthy company culture than owners of businesses that are solely revenue-driven and not interested in doing "good" in the world. It's kind of hokey and overly simplistic to label businesses as "good" (and don't get me wrong, I'm not saying that businesses focused on steep financial goals are "bad"), but what I'm talking about are businesses that are particularly forward-thinking, creative, and focused on making an impact on the world. These kinds of nonprofits, creative agencies, and innovative organizations are a different class of business than companies only driven by revenue-based metrics.

One of the biggest differences these businesses face is that employees tend to be very dedicated to the work of a company they believe in. This can be amazing for creating focus, motivation, and drive. But it can also contribute to toxic company culture. The reason is that no employee wants to be the one who sticks out and drags down the team by complaining. Employees want to prove they are useful and that they care about work they know is making a difference in the world. That means that it is more likely that "good" companies won't find out about cultural health problems in a company until they have become so intolerable that employees are at a crisis.

Think about this: You work in the warehouse of a big box-store corporation. Down the street are three other companies just like it. You go to work every day at 7:00 a.m., and you unload supplies from a truck and load them onto shelves in the warehouse. One day, a co-worker says, "Women shouldn't be allowed to work in the warehouse." You consider your options, and you decide that even if HR doesn't like your complaint and fires you, you can get another job down the street at one of the other box stores. So, you go into the HR office and make your complaint.

Now, consider a different scenario: You just got your dream job at a non-profit advocating for youth with disabilities in the education system. You work any hours you are needed because you are so passionate about the work. A co-worker comes up to you and says, "Women shouldn't be allowed to work as advocates." You consider whether to tell your boss, but you feel embarrassed about complaining about such an ignorant comment when there are really more important things everyone sees in the office every day. You think about the kids you're advocating for, and you decide just to brush it off. You're tougher than that anyway. The comments keep coming and keep coming until one day, your co-worker undermines you to a school, and you feel you can't do your job anymore. So, you quit, and, still embarrassed that you couldn't cut it, you tell your boss that the work was just getting to you and you need a break.

Obviously, not every scenario is that straightforward, but the point is that employees who are just going to work for a paycheck they could get anywhere else are more motivated to report workplace issues because, among other reasons, they are not worried about distracting from important work. Employees who feel they couldn't get another similar job, and who want to focus on work they care about, are more likely to try to ignore a problem until it gets so bad that it feels intolerable.

So, owners of businesses doing good in the world have some unique and additional challenges in creating healthy company culture that differ from most employers, and it is not a challenge everyone wants to take on. Of course, most employers do not want to face the expense of high turnover or lawsuits, but beyond that, some employers are content to let employees struggle as they learn how to navigate office politics and even bullying. Some employers are too uncomfortable themselves with the ideas of discrimination, bullying, and harassment to consider taking an active role in creating a healthy workplace. Many don't want to hear complaints from employees. The problem with this is that it leaves the company vulnerable to crisis. You can't fix a problem that you don't know about.

The Healthy Company Culture

Since you are reading this book, I imagine it is different for you. I hope it is different for you. You may, like most of us, feel uncomfortable thinking about harassment and discrimination, but creating a healthy workplace culture is important enough to keep trying, even when it's uncomfortable. You have probably experienced what it's like to work in a company culture where you felt afraid and threatened versus a culture that felt safe and challenging. You understand how much more productive, creative, and focused employees can be when they are in a healthy workplace culture. You may even, like me, have had the experience of working late into the night with someone else because it's fun. (What can I say? Some of us are addicted to work.)

But, wanting to create a healthy workplace culture and actually knowing how to create it are two different things. First, you have to decide what it even means to you to have a healthy workplace culture. To me, it means creating a safe place for people to have very different perspectives, experiences, and contributions. It means conflict will come up sometimes, but with the underlying expectation that everyone involved act with respect. It means everyone in the workplace understands why they are there and wants to contribute. It means not just giving people of all types, including people of color, of all genders and gender backgrounds, of all sexual orientations, all abilities, of all religions and nationalities the opportunity to participate, but actually including them and valuing respectful viewpoints that are unpopular or different than our own. It means that there is enough security and respect (both respect of others and self-respect) for people to truly be creative, seek challenge, and embrace failure as a crucial part of growth.

We all have a role in creating a culture that fosters discrimination, and some believe harassment and discrimination are acceptable (at least in some circumstances) or are unsure how to identify it. For example, the Olympics and the NBA intentionally maintain standards that naturally exclude many people with disabilities and segregate between the sexes. They can define what an inclusive environment looks like to them, within those parameters, but some groups will still find them exclusive. It can be different to create an "inclusive" or "healthy" environment than to create a "diverse" environment. My definition above includes both, but not every work environment chooses both, and it is important to make a deliberate choice about that with legal advice.

The tools in this book can be used for workplaces that are not diverse, like those that are, but it is important to keep in mind that diverse workplaces have been shown to be more effective and successful than homogenous ones. I believe the tools in this book can help promote inclusive and diverse workplaces.

When a workplace is culturally healthy, it can create magic. This is because respectful, diverse opinions allow for creativity and growth that is not available in other environments.

Most business owners do not start their business with the hopes of babysitting high-conflict, high-drama employees. There's no sense in pretending anything different. But, as your business starts to scale and expand, you are statistically likely to have incidents of conflict and even harassment and discrimination. The research indicates that hiring the "right" people may be an impossible goal, and it is at least much costlier than healing the cultural wounds your company has now.

We often think, if someone has a good business and is doing good work in the world, they won't have discrimination or harassment in their company. But, really, I have seen non-profits doing incredible work shut down over harassment and discrimination allegations; I have seen artistic companies with incredibly high turnover as a result of abusive management behavior; I have seen law firms who could barely manage because of staff gossip; and we have all seen people we respected accused of sexual assault or harassment.

Being able to do your job well does not necessarily mean you have learned the skills of handling high-conflict, high-drama situations at work. They are separate skills. We often believe that a "good person" will know how to respond to harassment or discrimination allegations and that only "bad people" struggle, but after having worked in this area for years, that is not my experience. Responding to high-conflict, high-drama situations at work or allegations of harassment, discrimination, or bullying is a skill that most of us have not been taught.

We would never expect a business owner to understand how to install her own electrical wiring or even cater the food at her own events. But we expect business owners to be able to navigate high-conflict situations with employees that involve sensitive cultural topics, even though they have never received information or training about how to do so. Some of these situations are as though there was an exposed electrical wire, and we expected the business owner to navigate rewiring their building with no expert advice. This sets the business owner up to make the situation much worse, sometimes dangerously so. This is often what I see as a lawyer who has spent years advocating for employees, and it's why in this book I want to share as much as I can about what I've seen work to solve these problems. Like with electrical wiring, there are solutions to make a workplace culturally healthy, and it does not take magic. It just takes the right tools.

The problem is that we have only recently come to understand (even in a limited way) the brain and the cognitive biases that create conflict around cultural differences. Even those of us who have been trained in traditional conflict resolution methods usually have not been trained in methods that effectively work where there are genuinely clashing cultural beliefs or extreme cultural betrayals. Instead, we are trained in negotiation and investigation methods that assume an even balance of power and promote competition for the win. I have heard mediators and seasoned attorneys talk about resolving a dispute as "getting to the deal in a used-car sale." That is not because they lack compassion, but because when we are dealing with strictly a legal claim, not the human reality of cultural conflict, money is usually all we have to deal with. A legal claim becomes some version of a used-car deal where both sides are just negotiating the financial value a jury might give.

There is nothing inherently bad about the legal system restricting negotiations to settling financial harms that can be repaired, but it does not do the additional work of repairing the cultural breakdown and the suffering around conflict that many employees experience day in and day out. The reality is that if we wait until there is a legal dispute to negotiate a resolution, which will inevitably be expensive and stressful, but really only address the financial component of the problem, it is a burden on both employers and employees.

Often good employers and their good employees face the costs of harassment and discrimination, rather than avoiding that cost by taking preventative measures or shifting the cost to the people accused of harassment and discrimination. I don't want that for you. There are not any other workplace issues I can think of where employers are so willing to front the financial costs of a preventable workplace hazard. The EEOC reported that in 2018 it recovered $70 million from employers through sexual harassment claims alone. The EEOC reports remarkably low settlement amounts compared to legal settlements, as well. (In one research project I did to prepare for mediation in two sexual harassment cases where I was representing the harassed women, I calculated that an average EEOC settlement was around $10,000 per complainant, but some looked much larger because there were often such a large group of complainants.) Most settlements where attorneys are involved tend to be much higher than an EEOC settlement. So, the $70 million figure likely represents a large number of complainants, rather than high settlement amounts. So, one business owner may pay a large settlement, and at the same time, each complainant against that business may get a small settlement. This seems like a lose-lose situation for both the business owner and the innocent employees who were harassed.

If you are not ready to embrace the challenge of being an inclusive leader who is willing to create a workplace that is safe and productive and also full of different perspectives, backgrounds, and cultural influences, that is totally your choice. This book may just help you resolve high-conflict employee disputes and respond to complaints of harassment and discrimination if and when things get bad.

Just remember, being inclusive is not only more fun, challenging, and interesting, it is also a good business decision. The reason is that when different cultures and opinions can come together and communicate, there is amazing magic and creativity. Companies that can represent a spectrum of perspectives can speak to clients and customers outside of the owner's circle. Businesses that value inclusion have the opportunity to surpass other businesses – for example, according to the Peterson Institute of International Economics, companies with more than thirty percent of women in leadership do consistently financially better than those with fewer women in leadership. Research from Goldman Sachs and USAID shows that countries with women in leadership have higher GDP. Diversity is good for problem solving, for reaching new audiences, and generally good for business. Even if you are starting with a homogenous workplace now, using the pillars of diagnosis, appropriate confidentiality, transparency, and power dynamics facilitation will make your workplace safer and more productive and set the groundwork to hire employees with diverse backgrounds and perspectives.

I break these pillars into three steps in this book. Each part is meant to lay out for you how to really put these steps into practice in your business, while considering your own industry and mission. I have seen business owners apply each of these steps differently based on their industry, and it is normal to work with a lawyer or power dynamics facilitator as you put them into practice for your unique business.

Step 1: Diagnosis. The first step is about diagnosing your company culture as it is now. In Chapter 3, we talk about situations of open conflict, where it is not necessary to perform formal diagnosis. This can often happen in workplaces with people of different backgrounds and beliefs, but it should be taken as a sign of potential growth, not a reason to resort to a homogenous workplace culture.

In Chapter 4, we talk about the first step I take business owners through in a Cultural Health Facilitation process, when there is not open conflict. This step is diagnosing where your culture is now through an effective Cultural Health Survey. Like we talked about above, the majority of incidents of harassment and discrimination go unreported. This is especially difficult in good companies, where employees don't want to distract from the work. Many business owners believe that because they have a good company doing good work in the world with good employees, they do not have to worry about cultural health problems. This is like saying, "I recycle and volunteer at church, so I won't get the flu this year." They are completely unrelated, and often, working for a company doing really great work in the world also has its own individualized challenges regarding cultural health issues, like I talked about earlier.

In order to address potential issues, rather than letting them fester, this step teaches you how to be proactive in seeking out any potential problems so that you can address them before they get bad. Remember, a survey gets you initial, basic, superficial information, but truly addressing cultural health requires much more.

Step 2: Confidential Reporting. In Step 2 we talk about the importance of confidential reporting options for situations where community danger is not an issue. I break this down into two considerations. First, in Chapter 4, I explain how to promote early reports. Most company cultural health issues go unreported, and employees have good reasons for not reporting.

A confidential reporting mechanism in every business, where possible, allows employees to seek advice and perspective on their situation, with protections around retaliation. If employees know that they can't seek advice about negative experiences they might be having without the conversation being repeated back to a harasser, they will not report, and you will never learn about the issues (or you will learn about them after they have gotten dangerous).

Offering a confidential reporting mechanism sometimes means having an external resource (a contracted lawyer or consultant) who is a reporting option, or sometimes it means having people designated within the company who are a safe reporting option.

Second, in Chapter 5, we talk about when investigations are appropriate. Sometimes, discipline is necessary around allegations and you have other employees and clients to protect, so full confidentiality is not required. In some situations, investigation can be necessary and we talk about how to know when that is.

Step 3: Power Dynamics. In Step 3 of the book (my favorite part!), we talk about the tools that I use to help employees shift power dynamics and create healthy workplace cultures. When an employee reports a cultural health problem, whether anonymously through a Cultural Health Survey or through another reporting mechanism, it is crucial to respond immediately and appropriately. Creating inclusion is not about listening to problems and doing nothing or finding out about problems and then retaliating against the reporter for talking about them. It is better to decide not to find out at all about the problems than to actively find out about them and retaliate or fail to respond.

In Chapter 6, we talk about the underlying cause of power imbalance at work and how I work with employees to repair unfairnesses and inequalities. When we can truly understand power dynamics and make the shifts necessary to create a healthy environment for ourselves at all times, we can effectively stop and prevent harassment and discrimination.

In Chapter 7, we talk about the root cause of high-crisis conflict and how to resolve it. Some people have been trained in a competitive, negotiation model of conflict resolution, while others believe strongly in a community-building model. Using power dynamics to resolve conflicts can acknowledge where both of these other models have strengths and tailor a resolution to the individual seeking it.

In Chapter 8, we talk about transparency in responding to conflict and cultural health issues at work. Transparency can create a structure where both the employer and employee have clear expectations, so that issues around pay, discipline, and termination, while still important and often hard, contain less crisis drama. For employers, transparency can help you know when discipline and termination are appropriate; for employees, transparency can reduce the perception of unfairness or give an opportunity to correct unfairness where it exists.

Each of us has her own feelings and sensitive points about these topics, and so I encourage you to be easy with yourself through this book and take breaks when they will serve you. It is okay to skip around if that serves you better, but I encourage you to allow discomfort to be okay. If something comes up for you about your own experience, let that discomfort exist. You are strong enough to feel difficult feelings. I know that for a fact if you have created a business. That is hard work! Ignoring this issue is like ignoring a broken leg. It might heal, but is that how you want it to heal?

Feeling difficult feelings and looking at the issue anyway is worth it for the future generations who will come after us, looking back and wondering why we did not practice mental hygiene and let so many die because of our unwillingness to practice regular mental hygiene. Honestly, though, I think these topics are incredibly freeing to talk about. I hate to be a downer about them, but I want you to know that if they are difficult for you, you are not alone. If you find it exciting to think of the possibility of a future where we have so mastered mental hygiene that every employee knows how to shift power dynamics to create a safe environment, you are also not alone in that. That is how I feel, and so I'm excited you're willing to listen to my lectures on the topic.

Thanks for making the world a better place!

Step 1: Diagnosis

Chapter 3: Open Conflict

When there is open conflict, unrest, or job insecurity in a workplace, diagnosis is not a mystery. The cultural health issues are loudly presenting themselves. But, often what we do instead of taking active steps to solve the problem is either give up or resort to extreme discipline or discharge of employees who seem like the "problem." This can create high turnover in businesses where employees have diverse backgrounds and beliefs, and the turnover often favors one particular viewpoint over others. The reason is that merely hiring a diverse workforce does not create an inclusive or healthy environment. Each person brings their history, beliefs, and traumas with them to the workplace, and often this can lead to at least tension, if not open fighting.

I do not mean to say that hiring employees with different backgrounds or belief systems automatically leads to crisis conflict. In fact, it more often leads to creativity and growth. I only mean to say that many business owners believe that merely the step of hiring people with different backgrounds will automatically create growth. That is not necessarily the case either, and it is important to be deliberate in allowing creativity and even conflict in your workplace culture. Diversity leads to growth because people are forced to be creative and see things from a new perspective. This is not always easy, and sometimes it leads to tension about sensitive topics. In this chapter, I specifically talk about our own biases and belief systems as they relate to crisis conflict, especially with opposing viewpoints, but this can exist no matter how homogenous a workplace appears.

When we have not been taught how to resolve conflict and shift power dynamics, as this book talks about more in Step 3, it can feel overwhelming to resolve the conflict created by openly clashing perspectives. In those situations, I sometimes see employers resort to layoffs or harsh discipline.

Instead, when an employer understands how to effectively respond to conflict created by clashing perspectives, it is possible to use that experience to create growth in the business.

Clashing Perspectives

Creating a diverse and inclusive workplace culture means you will run into clashing viewpoints. When I am at speaking events, I often get questions like, "What about people who are just misunderstanding and unreasonably interpreting innocent behavior as harassment?" or, "How is your process going to help me know who is right and who is lying?" People (men and women) remind me that the accused are "innocent until proven guilty, so how do we balance that with supporting victims and not go too far?"

On the other hand, you may have followed social media hashtags like #MeToo, #TimesUp, #BelieveHer, and #SayHerName, which are strongly advocating for a shift in how we listen to stories about violence against women. There is a dramatic polarization right now in culture in the United States between those who want to focus on evidence and proof and those who believe that much of the discrimination people face does not get recorded into evidence but is still devastating our country and holding huge amounts of our population back.

Our brains have evolved to protect us from predators like mountain lions, and so they tend to see these conflicts as life-threatening crises. Our brains say, "Someone who looks like you has been hurt and you could be hurt next! Protect yourself!" We see a man like Brett Kavanaugh, Al Franken, or Harvey Weinstein challenged in his position, and we think, "My husband, son, brother, or I could be challenged in the roles we have worked for." We see a woman like Christine Blasey Ford, Leann Tweeden, or Rose McGowan tell her story, and we think, "My wife, daughter, sister, or I could be in physical danger from a man and it seems like there's nothing we can do about it." And because we don't see anything we can do about the issue that seems like the biggest threat to us, our brains shut down and we become hopeless and defensive. People on both sides of the debate start to believe that even talking about harassment and discrimination is a threat.

The statistics and research reflect that men are still a leading cause of death to women in the United States. It also shows that police use of deadly force is dramatically disproportionate against black people than white people and white people are a major cause of death for black people. It is no surprise then that the hashtags #AllLivesMatter and #NotAllMen in response to those who tell their stories of harassment, discrimination, and violence sound like saying #MountainLionsMatter and #NotAllMountainLions to a victim of mountain lion attacks.

At the same time, the research and statistics do show that it is not a majority of men or a majority of white people committing active violence against women and black people. (Likewise, I want to mention, as a nod to the wildlife advocates out there, that an even larger majority of mountain lions have not attacked humans this year.) Many of us feel defensive that we have not committed acts of violence, and so we want to defend that we are "not bad." We believe that those who have committed violence are "bad people" and those of us who have not can still be "good people," and we don't want to be lumped into the pile of bad apples and cut off from our community.

Now, I am not speaking to those who openly embrace the role of predator and believe that their job is to wipe out populations who are not like them. I am speaking to those who genuinely do not want to see violence happen, no matter whom they see as the instigator. We do not have to identify as "sexist," "racist," "ableist," "homophobic," "transphobic," or "xenophobic" for example, or be that in our souls, in order to say something that contributes to discrimination. Many of us want to be inclusive leaders, but we also don't want to be "PC police" or even get involved where we could hurt others with our ignorance.

Often, when faced with high-crisis conflicts like these, what we think we want is for everyone to suddenly realize our one perspective is right and change their minds to agree with us. That is not bad in and of itself, and obviously each of us thinks our perspective is right or we would change our minds (and be right again). There is some satisfaction in believing we are right and a whole group of other people is wrong. It often seems like the only other options are indifference, which feels terrible, or pretending to agree with the other side, which seems fake and weak. Those are not good options, and so we become more and more entrenched in our own perspectives. We have our team, and the other side has their team, and we both ridicule and yell at each other from across the football field.

These are *not* the only options, though.

If you really do believe that inclusion, equality, justice, and fairness are important values, your workplace deserves better than the war paint of the football field. If you believe that creating a culture based on integrity, grit, creativity, and skill is a worthy goal, then treating it like a game, where we can all have the bad behavior of children, is disrespectful to that goal.

So, when one-person posts #BelieveWomen and another person responds with #NotAllMen, how do you prevent your business from becoming a warzone and your employees from getting completely derailed from their actual jobs? When employees with socially disadvantaged characteristics are seeing employees with privilege as though they are the mountain lion, how do you create a safe environment that lets everyone work productively?

The answer I teach in this book is that we need to understand power dynamics and how our thinking contributes to imbalanced power dynamics at work. When you can teach your employees to effectively understand and shift power dynamics (and when you can understand them yourself), you can help employees create safety, appreciate that safety, and focus on the work they are in your business to do.

I mean no disrespect when I make this analogy, but I believe that our work to learn about discrimination and bias now is like 150 years ago when people were first learning that germs kill people. There were some doctors who did not believe in germs and insisted on performing surgeries without washing their hands. There were others who kind of believed germs existed, but they argued that they had washed their hands once, so they shouldn't have to wash their hands again before surgery. There were others who were pioneers, who insisted on consistent hygiene, and it's these doctors who saved patients' lives.

What we are facing with inclusion and cultural health issues now is the same situation but related to our mental health and our cognitive biases. The reality is that all brains have cognitive biases, like all hands have germs. We need to practice consistent mental hygiene like we practice hygiene around germs. This means we need to actively look at and question our thoughts, like I describe later in this book.

Ignoring discrimination and harassment does not make it go away any more than ignoring germs makes them go away. People die in the United States every day because we do not have routine mental health regimens around the biases in our brains – because we allow discrimination to continue. When we look back now on the people who died in surgery because a doctor didn't wash his hands, it seems like a completely preventable tragedy. The same is true for the deaths of women in the United States because they were denied reproductive health care or of black people and Muslims who are being killed. A decade from now, when we have mastered mental hygiene, we will look back on these deaths as tragically preventable.

Like with germs in the nineteenth century, the problems around discrimination today often do not look like one evil person setting out to destroy someone else. Many people wrongly believe that we are solidly on the side of equality if we haven't punched a black person, gay person, or a woman today. We say, "Look, that business employs black people, so it must not be discriminatory." This is like saying a doctor did not contribute to unsanitary conditions in hospitals unless he deliberately put dirt in a patient's wound. Each of us contributes, whether positively or negatively, to the systems that promote people to privileged positions or prevent them from getting there.

This is true for the discrimination we experience against ourselves as much as the discrimination we see against others. When you have a employees who believe abusive or discriminatory things *about themselves* that alone can contribute to crisis conflict. Our unconscious and conscious biases contribute to our willingness to do uncomfortable, hard things and stretch ourselves to see new perspectives. It is always possible to examine our thinking, practice mental hygiene, and contribute to a more productive, inclusive, culturally healthy workplace that we will benefit from as much as anyone else.

Opportunity *and* Inclusion

Many employers believe they are working toward solving discrimination by simply hiring a "diverse" workforce, and that is a great first step. Most of the early legal work in Civil Rights has also been to provide opportunities to groups with disadvantaged characteristics so that they have the opportunity to participate in areas they had been banned from (for example, owning property, having careers, and voting). The problem we've seen with this is that it is one thing to hire a person of color into a job, but it is an entirely different thing to keep her and allow her to advance in her position. It is one thing to say, "I've given this employee the opportunity to do well in his job, now it's on him to take it." It's a different matter entirely to create an inclusive, culturally healthy workplace environment. Most of us want to have a healthy workplace, but when we run into signs of un-health, we try to hide them and cover them up, rather than diagnose and treat the wound. Just like when a physical wound goes ignored and untreated, at best this leads to scarring, at worst it leads to an infection that can destroy the entire system.

We often misuse the term "diverse" and use it to mean "member of a disadvantaged group." The most common example of this is when someone calls a job candidate a "diverse" candidate, meaning the candidate has disadvantaged characteristics, like being a woman, a person of color, homosexual, transgender, differently abled, Muslim, etc. Really, a workplace that is all women is as homogenous as a workplace that is all men. A workplace that is all black people is as homogenous as a workplace that is all white people. Each of those lacks diversity. Some business owners may deliberately choose that for conscious reasons and with legal advice, but often discriminatory hiring decisions are illegal.

We know that having a diverse workforce contributes to success. But, if we are going to have both a diverse and healthy workplace cultures, it means we will have people who don't understand each other and people who don't understand what it means to be discriminatory. This does not have to be unsafe or threatening if we are willing to communicate, empower employees to set and enforce boundaries, and teach people tools that work to stop harassing and discriminatory behavior.

One of the ways navigating discrimination law in a crisis situation as an employer becomes tricky is that many employees believe discrimination and harassment is completely illegal at all times. Others believe the law only protects people with traditionally disadvantaged characteristics (i.e. women not men). Most employers know that neither question is that simple. In fact, most harassment and discrimination is actually legal, and the law only prohibits it in certain limited instances. For example, with sexual harassment, in most cases it is only illegal if it happens at work and is severe or pervasive, offensive to a reasonable person in that situation, and unwanted. Think about the level harassment has to reach in order for the average person to consider it severe or pervasive. It then, as a practical matter, often has to affect some kind of tangible part of an employee's job (e.g., forcing them to lose pay or requiring medical treatment) in order for the law to step in. For the most part, unless harassment rises to that level or higher, the law is not interested in it. But, the vast majority of harassment is at least disrespectful, unacceptable behavior at work that does not rise to the level of affecting someone's pay or requiring medical attention.

In some ways, this standard disadvantages business owners as much as it disadvantages employees. It sends the message that, as a society, we don't actually care that much about harassment and discrimination, and that even though stealing *any* amount of money is considered illegal theft, harassment is only "real" if it's so severe or pervasive that anyone would consider it intolerable. This encourages employers not to care about their company culture and to treat it as unimportant, when in reality company culture determines how much brain space and energy employees are able to put in to their work. It misleads business owners into thinking that creating a diverse and inclusive workplace culture is about being nice instead of a crucial business decision to stay competitive in your industry.

On the other hand, it is not necessarily the law's place to step in with every harassing situation, and in some ways that can be disempowering to the workplace culture for the law to be the only go-to solution. This is similar to an employer trying to solve an employee's problems for her. I often see with business owners that if they could, they would solve every problem for their employees. If you ever find yourself texting employees at night about their roommate problems or boyfriend drama, you are not alone. If you've ever wanted to shake an employee for not believing in themselves enough and force them to be more confident with clients, you're also not alone. And, there are some situations where it is totally appropriate for you or the law to step in and address the problem. There are other situations where solving it for an employee disempowers them. Teaching employees how to stop behaviors they find offensive, giving them permission to do that, and supporting respectful interactions empowers employees to create a self-sustaining healthy culture.

It might sound overwhelming to consider dealing with harassment, discrimination, or bullying allegations, and many business owners give up and fire everyone when these issues come up. (It might sound like I'm exaggerating or joking, but I'm not.) This is similar to how your employees may try to ignore and minimize the impact of bullying until it gets worse and worse before they quit. If you've said to an employee before, "I think that's just his personality," "I think she meant it as a joke," or "That sounds like a misunderstanding," you are not alone, and this is one way that our brains try to ignore harassment and discrimination. We often think the alternative to ignoring and minimizing is for everyone to freak out, conduct a huge investigation, and burn the office down. Like I'll talk about more in this book, those are not the only options.

In reality, harassment and discrimination are incredibly common. If you can understand that and expect to encounter harassment and discrimination, it is easier to find a middle ground of practical steps to stopping it. When a problem is widespread, ignoring it or minimizing it doesn't help it go away, but freaking out and burning everything down doesn't help either.

Creating an inclusive, healthy workplace culture doesn't mean you have to fire all of your employees and go hire people who are somehow perfect and understand how to always be respectful. It doesn't mean that no hugs are allowed or that everyone has to intuitively understand cultural perspectives that are different than their own without asking any questions. It means that you empower employees with tools that work (in Step 3) so that they can engage in making the workplace healthy and productive. It means that employees know what to do when another person in the workplace does something they find offensive, without it having to become a trauma experience. It means that you may have employees who express discriminatory, harassing, bullying, or otherwise unacceptable behavior, and that other employees know how to stop that behavior without internalizing it.

Understanding the Inclusive Leader's Power

The trouble can become, though, that you, as a human, have your own beliefs, values, and even unconscious expectations of how life should be and how we should treat each other. It is just as easy for you to jump into the pit with the employees and expect your own perspective to be recognized and validated. Unfortunately, the more we expect other people to understand our perspective, the more we retreat to our own corners, from which we yell at and alienate people on the other side(s).

And, I'm sure you would be the first to admit that, like everyone else, you have your own biases, experiences, and areas of privilege. I know "privilege" can be a charged word, and so I want to take a moment to sit with that word. Many of us, when we hear the word "privilege," think of a person laying on a couch eating bonbons and watching Real Housewives all day long. "Wouldn't it be nice to be privileged?" we think, comparing that to our own struggles. But, also, it wouldn't be nice – because when someone points out our privilege, many of us feel like we've been accused of being a mountain lion that has attacked a group of hikers. We aren't violent and evil, we know, and so we can't be privileged. You may already do this, but I want to ask you to think about privilege a little differently than that, and hopefully in a way that better serves you. Privilege happens when we are raised in a culture that values a characteristic we naturally possess over other versions of that characteristic. For example, in a culture that values blond hair, believing that blond-haired people are better at math and science than brown, black, purple, or red-haired people, the blond-haired people hold a privilege. Those of us who hold privileges also usually have the privilege of not recognizing or being aware of our privilege. We feel "normal," not favored. Then, most of us have other, non-privileged characteristics where we can see that other people are unfairly favored over us in society. Holding a privilege does not in itself mean you have done something unfair, it means you have a place of leverage and power that is magical. It means you pulled at least one winning lottery ticket from life, and so you have the opportunity to think carefully about how to use that and how to honor it. Having a privilege is something to be proud of and also something to take seriously. It is nothing to be ashamed of and it does not negate the other areas where you may be unfairly disadvantaged.

You have your own perspective, and you can't know or even understand every other person's perspective. It is not necessarily your job to do that. But, just being an employer puts you in a position of power and privilege.

For example, many business advisors encourage companies to have "company values," and to separate any employee who does not adhere to these values. While there is nothing inherently wrong with having mission statements (or even company values) that help employees understand the core direction of the company, this can be a tricky cultural area. And, it is a lot of power to be able to separate an employee who disagrees with you. Even where different cultures discover that they ultimately have shared values of community and caring, almost every community expresses them in very different words and symbols. When I am talking about different cultures and communities, I do not mean only different races or ethnicities. This is as ubiquitous as thinking about how, when someone in New York tries to sell something to a person in Des Moines, there is a cultural divide. When someone from a small town in the US tries to work for a company in a large city, there is a major cultural shift. Our "company values" show our cultural biases, for better or for worse. When we are trying to create an inclusive company culture, that is often in contradiction with the idea of firing anyone who does not follow our company values.

We can't see our own cognitive biases, stereotypes, or personal expectations. When we are writing our own company values and mission statement, it is supposed to come from the business owner's vision and brain. The challenge then, as a business owner who has her own values and mission, is to let yourself listen to other cultures, other biases, and other opinions that are different from yours.

The same is true when you are navigating employee conflict. If you choose to be the one to resolve employee conflict, in order to really address the root issues in the conflict, it is important to be aware and do your own work on your privileges and biases so that you are able to create a safe space for the resolution. You are not always the right person to do that, and that is completely normal.

Sometimes your own biases or privileges will make it difficult for you to see or understand when someone with a different perspective is experiencing something they believe to be conflict or even something they believe to be harassing or discriminatory. If you are experiencing open conflict, and you are ready to find out how to deal with it, you can skip right to Step 3, which talks about how to effectively respond. If you, like so many employers, are concerned that your own perspective might be making it difficult for you to see when your employees are experiencing your work environment differently than you, Chapter 4 discusses how to take an active role in diagnosing your company culture.

Takeaways

- Diverse workplace culture contributes to better success in business.
- Sometimes diverse perspectives can lead to open conflict.
- As a business owner, you have your own privileges and biases, and those are something to honor, not something to be ashamed of.
- You are not the right person to resolve conflict if you want your employees to change their perspectives and agree with you. This is okay, and there are other options.

Chapter 4: Cultural Health Survey

Most of us have had this experience:

Your friend asks you, "How are you doing?"

You reply, "Fine." (You mean, "Not fine. I'm having a major problem," which your friend should gather by the tone of your voice.)

Your friend moves on to talk about whatever he wanted to talk about, which is inevitably something stupid (especially compared to what is going on with you).

Your friend becomes a former friend, at least in your mind. </scene>

Now, we are not always friends with our employees, and many business owners maintain a deliberate professional, not personal, relationship with employees. But, the principle of the "I'm fine" conversation translates nevertheless to employer/employee relationships. The reason is that both employees and employers are humans, with human lives, human interests, human emotions, and human problems. We have to want to hear about a problem in order to hear about it. We can believe we are listening, but unless we are actively taking steps to find out about a problem, we often miss it.

When you hire someone to do a job for you, you probably just want that person to *do their job* so that you don't have to worry about doing it. Those of us who have trained another person know it is not that simple. We invest more at the outset in training a new employee in order to save countless hours and allow company growth later – that is the tradeoff. The same is true with finding out about cultural health problems employees are experiencing. It is an initial investment and effort that has the potential to lead to tremendous productivity later.

Long Term Efficiency

When I was first hired as a new associate, working for a law firm, I had previous experience managing groups of employees in retail, teaching forty Ukrainian fifth graders in a classroom, and as a legal assistant myself. I had been in situations where I needed to advocate for myself and others in front of much more experienced, powerful people. But I had not run into the particular situation I encountered (it wasn't sexual harassment; don't worry, this one's different).

My new assistant was an incredibly experienced, knowledgeable, and detailed person. She was also one of the sweetest people you will ever meet. She had at least thirty more years of experience (in everything) than I did, and she had assisted respected attorneys and judges in our community for decades, working on cases that made huge impacts in the law.

I was new, and it was a challenge for us to navigate the difference between the instructions I gave her that were strange to her because I was just wrong and the instructions that were strange to her because they intentionally used new technology or strategies. I became frustrated when she would follow her routine practices, rather than making the shifts I asked for.

I was at a conference with a coaching colleague when my assistant sent an email following a routine practice that I thought I had asked her to suspend for a particular client. I explained to the colleague, "It just seems so inefficient for me to keep having to ask over and over again for these changes, when I don't feel like she understands the reason for them."

"What if it's not supposed to be efficient?" My colleague asked.

That question blew my mind. To me, everything about having an assistant was supposed to be about efficiency. My work was supposed to be more productive and happen more quickly because of the second person working on it.

"What if your experience with your assistant is about you becoming a compassionate leader in every situation, starting with this small situation?" my colleague asked.

At first, I hated this idea.

After I adjusted to it, though, I started to see how it served me better than just being frustrated all the time. I started to consider whether every interaction with my assistant, whether she understood my instructions or not, could be a gift and opportunity for me to learn how to lead another truly incredible person. The very fact that she knew more than me most of the time, but I was the one responsible for the outcome in each case, created an environment in which we both had to learn how to communicate clearly and respectfully.

I became grateful for our miscommunications (which happened less and less) as part of the obstacle course that was training me to become a leader.

Now, don't get me wrong, I believe in efficiency. Like most humans, my brain is wired with what Dr. Douglas Lisle calls the Motivational Triad. The Motivational Triad describes that our brains are unconsciously focused on conserving energy, seeking pleasure, and avoiding pain. Our brains evolved while we were running from giant predators (like the good ol' mountain lion who I've been giving so much flack in this book) and surviving through cold winters on scarce resources. The Motivational Triad exists for good reason and allowed our ancestors to survive. Efficiency conserves energy, and so it seems just plain good to the unconscious, primitive parts of our brains. And, while efficiency is not actually bad, short-term efficiency can actually create long-term problems when it undermines the cultural health of a business.

It may sound like I am saying that I was willing to sacrifice my law practice and the clients I was so passionate about serving so that my assistant could feel comfortable and refuse to follow my instructions. That is *not* what I'm saying. My work and my clients were still my number one priority. I also did not have to sacrifice my assistant in order to achieve long-term efficiency, though.

What I am saying is that both are possible.

Often business owners make the mistake of believing they have to find all of the "right" people for each job position, and that if there is an interpersonal problem, they have found the "wrong" people (or at least one "wrong" person). This "bad apple" assumption can cost companies thousands of dollars. We have to remember that it costs around one-fifth of an employee's salary to replace that employee. If we assume that when a problem happens, we have the wrong people working for us, the hiring process can become a money pit.

The reality is that cultural health issues happen in good companies, with good employees. The business owners who create cultural health do so by taking deliberate steps to create cultural health, not by firing employees at the first sign of trouble. In fact, high turnover is almost certain to contribute to increasing harassment and discrimination, not reducing it.

Asking Questions

The first step in creating cultural health is diagnosing the health status of the current culture. When I took more time to sit with my assistant and figure out what was going on with our miscommunications, I found areas where I could improve in communication and areas where she was experiencing anxiety that I could help alleviate. Before you can work toward creating permanent cultural health in your company, you need to know whether your company needs to take some vitamin C to prevent a small cold, or whether you are facing a systemic cancer and a chemo-like treatment is necessary. Are you taking preventative measures or does your company culture need emergency surgery?

If your company's culture is truly toxic, a Band-Aid is not going to work. But there is no need to go under anesthesia if your business's culture is facing a small conflict that could be easily solved.

From working as a lawyer representing employees in harassment and discrimination lawsuits, I started to realize how much difference it can make for a company to ask the right questions. I realized after a few years of practice that when I would first meet a potential client and hear about a problem, I would ask very different questions than companies were asking.

I found out that HR departments and business owners often asked questions like, "Couldn't this be a misunderstanding?" and "Are you sure he meant it that way?" and "What proof do you have of that?" and my favorite, "Do you want to initiate a formal investigation?" (Hint: Zero people want to initiate a formal investigation. All people want to feel safe and respected at work.)

The questions tended to make sense to an outside person, but there was one very important problem with them from a legal perspective – they were cross-examination questions. Often companies were cross-examining employees before they asked direct examination questions.

Direct examination is, in trial, where an attorney tries to get out all of the information that the witness wants to say. We ask open-ended questions, and it is almost always (though not always) the attorney who is on the side of the witness who asks the questions. The purpose is to tell the jury all the reasons the witness is right.

Cross examination is, in trial, where the opposing attorney gets to try to prove the witness wrong (or at least lead the witness in a particular direction). We ask leading questions and try to get the witness to agree to them.

When a business owner does not want to find out about a cultural health issue, she is likely to ask leading cross-examination questions when an employee comes to her. This does not make the business owner a bad person necessarily, but it doesn't get her good information either.

The reason this happens is generally because of two important thinking errors that all of our brains have. The first is the "halo effect" and the second is confirmation bias.

The halo effect happens when I see someone do one thing I believe is good, and so I believe everything he does is good. If I see someone do well at playing with his child, the halo effect is likely to make me think everything else he does is good. We know hypothetically that someone can play with a child one day and also commit a crime the next. But, when confronted with that idea, it challenges my bias.

Confirmation bias happens when we have a belief and then we notice all of the evidence that exists to support that belief, and none of the evidence that contradicts it. If I believe my work colleague is a great guy and a model father, for example, and someone comes to me and tells me that he harassed her, it goes against my belief that he is a great guy and a model father. I may reject that complaint because of my own confirmation bias. Instead, I am likely to look for evidence that will confirm my bias. I will ask questions like, "Well, don't you think you're taking that wrong?" because I am looking for evidence of what I already believe.

In order for a business owner to get good information about her company's cultural health, she has to take deliberate steps to look for that information that goes against her natural assumptions. Because of the halo effect, she might assume that if she has a good company that is doing important things in the world, all of her employees are happy too, even though the two are unrelated. The reality is that often good companies face more difficult challenges in maintaining healthy culture. Once she has a particular belief, though, she will continue to see evidence of it because of confirmation bias.

Employees are unlikely to come to her directly because they want to prove they are good workers and care about the good work of the company, but even if they do, it is a tremendous challenge to overcome that kind of confirmation bias.

In order to create a culturally healthy work environment, you have to *want* to find out about problems and actively diagnose them. That is easier said than done, and so I want to walk you through a few steps to develop a culture in which it comes naturally to you to *want* to hear about problems.

First, Decide What You Want to Know

I am not going to walk you through exactly how to create your own Cultural Health Survey because there are so many different practical ways that it can work. You could send a text message or an email with the right questions. You could use a form like Google Surveys, Survey Monkey, or WuFoo. You could do a Facebook poll if that's the way that is easiest for you to communicate with your people. However, an anonymous survey is always going to get you better information than one that requires employees to identify themselves with their answers.

We often spend a lot of time wanting our communications to *look* good, but that makes no difference if you don't know what information you are looking for and what information you don't want to know.

Traditional employee surveys take about four forms: health surveys, engagement surveys, violence surveys, and safety surveys. Each of these formats has benefits. For example, the questions about positive reinforcement, transparency, challenge, and communication in the traditional engagement surveys can give a company great information about whether an employee is likely to stay in her position. Questions about whether on-the-floor employees observe any hazards and have equipment necessary to do their jobs can give important information about immediate dangers in the workplace.

We are still navigating how to ask employees about cultural hazards though, and many surveys have shown to be very ineffective in asking the right questions. For example, health surveys tend to ask employees questions like, "How often do you exercise?" and "Do you smoke?" These are not bad questions on their face, but they do put the employee on the defensive and tend to sound like, "Are you trying hard enough? Are you a broken piece of equipment?" More importantly, though, they do not ask questions about the cultural experience of the workplace, only the physical health of the employee.

Worse, violence surveys ask questions like, "Have you experienced sexual harassment at work?" Again, this question is not bad on its face, but it has been shown to be incredibly ineffective. The reason is that no one knows what "sexual harassment" means. When a survey asks about components of sexual harassment (e.g. "Have you been exposed to sexual images or conversation at work in a way that made you uncomfortable?" or "Have you been touched at work in a way that made you uncomfortable?") responses have been shown to be enormously higher than with general questions about "sexual harassment."

The first step in creating an effective Cultural Health Survey (which is just a fancy name I am using for asking your employees the right questions to get the information you want about a problem) is to decide (1) the problems you do want to find out about, and (2) the problems you do not want to find out about (if any).

If you only want to know if you are about to be sued, for example, you can phrase questions like, "Have you experienced discrimination at work?"

If you want to know whether your employees feel safe, though, it is important to be much more specific and also gentler in questions. For example, "In the past year, has anyone touched you in a way that made you uncomfortable at work?" will not tell you whether that touching qualifies for protection under discrimination law, but it will give you more information about whether your employee feels safe. You are more likely to get a higher number of "yes" responses to the second question than the first because people are reluctant to identify behavior as discriminatory until it has gotten very bad.

Here are a few questions that might help you identify what you do and do not want to know from a survey:

- Do you want to know whether employees feel respected at work?
- Do you want to know whether employees feel physically safe at work?
- Do you want to know whether employees like their jobs?
- Do you want to know whether employees feel secure in their jobs?
- Do you want to know whether employees will stay in their jobs long term or feel they have to transition to another job in order to advance their careers?
- Do you want to know whether employees are likely to engage in discriminatory or harassing behavior?
- Do you want to know whether employees feel financially secure in their positions?
- Do you want to know whether employees are experiencing anything that might violate employment law right now?

If you don't want to know the answers to any of these questions, the good news is you don't have to do anything! Just keep going on as things are and don't send out any surveys.

If you do want to know the answers to these questions, the thing to know is that it may give you something you actually need to effectively address. Even silence gives you information you may need to address. For example, if a large portion of employees with one characteristic do not respond to a survey, it is fair to take a negative response from this lack of response. These employees want to focus on work and do not want to "rock the boat" with their opinions about workplace cultural health, which are likely negative. One of the reasons most companies do not ask questions that are actually likely to get information about a company's cultural health is that they are worried that if they know, they will have to take action to correct the problem. Many business owners view this as "too hard." They don't want to know about problems because they don't want to have to do something about them.

The trouble with that thinking is that it can be much costlier and more time consuming to have high turnover and lawsuits than to correct a cultural health issue that will make employees more effective and efficient in the long term. At best, a cultural health issue can be like each of your employees having a pebble in her shoe while she works – it is distracting but manageable. At worst, it can be like your employee having a broken leg at work – it requires time off, constant management, and puts her in pain all day. Cultural health issues at work can absorb the majority of an employee's energy, leaving very little for her work. Most of us have been through heartbreak or challenges that suck our energy from work, so we can understand how much energy it takes to deal with an emotional experience. If you have an employee who is not meeting her potential, it is important to consider that a cultural health issue could be sucking her energy away from work through no fault of her own.

In order to craft your own questions to create the answers you want, here's a hack: Write out the answers you want to get *before* you write the questions. For example, if the answer you are looking for is, "One of my coworkers is super creepy and treating me differently because I'm Hispanic," what do you need to ask to get that answer? If the answer you are looking for is, "I have a disability that is not being accommodated," what do you need to ask in order to make sure you get that answer? The key may seem obvious, but it is that you have to ask a question that opens the door to those answers and allows them to be acceptable.

In the Cultural Health Survey I offer to employers, I use a Likert scale (meaning a scale that allows employees to respond with a range of one to four with one meaning "not at all like me" and four meaning "very like me") and I allow employees to respond to prompts like, "My race is respected at work" or "My gender is respected at work" to elicit direct answers about discrimination issues. I also allow them to respond to prompts like, "I love the people I work with," "I am uncomfortable around people at work," or "I know how to stop inappropriate behavior at work." I evaluate each of these scores and graph them so that an employer knows where employees are having an overall positive or overall negative experience at work, but also where there are targeted red-flag issues that may be an indicator of illegal discrimination. In every survey I have conducted so far, there have been a range of responses and a handful of employees who fall within a crisis level of response. There have also been a portion of employees who have not responded, indicating more room to create a safe space to talk about cultural health issues and prioritize those discussions.

Many lawyers may advise you to avoid asking questions that are going to get you those answers. This is because if you find out there is a problem and you *don't* effectively respond to it, your situation becomes way worse. This is good advice, and if you have an attorney, you should listen to your attorney.

But the tough thing is that if you want to have a culturally healthy workplace, you need to know about problems before they become intolerable. Because you're reading this book, my guess is that you are willing to do what it takes to create cultural health, even if it's hard. If you are ready to start healing cultural wounds in your workplace, you *have* to be willing to hear that they are there. There is no other way to heal them. Ignoring them does not make them go away. At the same time, you don't want to force employees to respond to these questions, which can also be abusive. The diagnosis portion is really to help you understand the problems employees are willing to voluntarily report and how many of your employees are not willing to report problems at all.

If you decide you are ready to really diagnose whether problems exist, the next decision you have to make is whether you want to develop your survey on your own or whether you want help. Either way, make sure your survey covers all characteristics protected by law and send it to all employees. Even if your workplace is racially homogenous (for example, all black), still ask questions that will get you information about whether people feel discriminated based on race and still send it to all employees. Even if your workplace is all women, still ask questions that will get you information about gender discrimination and send it to everyone, including yourself. Ask questions about all protected characteristics and send it to all people because if you exclude one, and there actually happens to be a problem related to that characteristic that you would never have thought of, leaving it out can make the problem even worse.

Second, Listen with Curiosity

The second step is to really listen with curiosity. Often, engaging in the first step and getting negative feedback can feel so overwhelming that particularly compassionate, empathetic employers shut down. This makes sense because we know how much time and energy we spend caring for our employees and worrying about them. To hear something negative from them can be intensely triggering. We know the sacrifices we make so that they can have a job and feed their family; we know the unpredictability of business income; we know which employees feel like an asset and which employees feel like a liability in our hearts. What if the negative feedback is just coming from whiners? Should we listen to that?

We don't want to hurt our employees. We don't want to be the bad guy. But some negative feedback just seems so unreasonable.

The question you need to ask yourself is whether it is worth it to you to find out about problems while they sound petty or unreasonable, so that you can prevent them from becoming systemic and fatal to your business.

A client who came to me to help her report sexual harassment worked for a non-profit that focused on advocating for a vulnerable population in the justice system. The work they were doing was important. I say "was" because the non-profit had no structure for diagnosing its own cultural health issues, even though it was active in advocating for others. Many women within the company felt they were experiencing harassment and discrimination, but by the time the board of directors found out about it, the issue was so pervasive and extreme that they had to shut the non-profit down. They lost the entire staff suddenly, although as far as I understand only my client was willing to say why, and because the director was the one accused of the harassment, the work couldn't continue. In my view, this was a great tragedy that could have been avoided by early diagnosis and simple preventative steps.

In order to be effective in truly diagnosing problems, a survey is only a first step. Even if you get responses in the survey that seem unreasonable or hurtful, you want to lean in to those responses and find out more (especially about the responses you want to resist). If you don't feel like the responses are comprehensive because a whole group of employees you want to listen to didn't respond, have compassion for your intention to listen, and listen to their silence.

Sometimes, business owners will want to break the anonymity of responses or target certain groups for follow-up based on what feels like genuine intent to listen. This can have disastrous consequences, though. A colleague shared with me that her company conducted a cultural health survey, which was supposed to be anonymous, but the director of a department forced the people conducting the survey to identify one of the employees based on a response. The director justified this, saying the response showed a misunderstanding the director wanted to clarify in order to help the employee. Because the anonymity was breached, however, it created rampant mistrust within the company and sent the message that employees could be targeted based on their responses. When I conduct a survey, the responses are anonymous, even to me.

People find direct pressure or singling out to answer the questions very intimidating and sometimes threatening (most people have experiences where they've been told if they talk about discrimination they'll get fired, and as I mentioned before, the EEOC reports that seventy-five percent of people who report discrimination experience retaliation). This step is intended to be a first note to say, "I care about your opinion if you want to share it," and to get you the information people are willing to share. Typical numbers for an employee survey response are sixty to ninety percent. Not filling it out is an answer in its own way even though it's not definitive.

For some people (this is true of me), asking them to fill out a cultural health survey is like saying, "we wanted to do a survey about how experiences of child abuse impacts your work." Then, for those who have not resolved their child abuse, just that question is intensely triggering. If you go back to them and say, "I notice you personally didn't tell us about your child abuse – please fill this out," any information you get is going to be informed by that person's experience of being singled out about their child abuse. It would be amazing instead to start working toward an environment where people can start to resolve those experiences and see that they're not dangerous to talk about.

If the majority of a culturally disadvantaged group doesn't respond to a survey, it makes sense. You could substitute "we're doing a survey about how being fat or thin impacts your work," and then if a majority of people classified as obese (the culturally disadvantaged characteristic) don't respond, it in itself provides some information. Having a skinny girl (or white person, man, able-bodied person, heterosexual, cis-gender, Christian, etc.) follow up individually and call people out for not responding won't increase people's sense of safety in responding. A cultural health survey is a very preliminary step and in itself does not resolve cultural health issues. Any information employees are willing to share is helpful in deciding next steps for moving forward, but the answers or lack of answers in themselves are only a first step.

To truly find out more about negative feedback and responses, you have to be able to manage and understand your own feelings and treat yourself like a good boss. After all, you are one of the employees of the company. This is a very challenging task.

To start, have compassion for your own feelings around the responses. It is impossible to listen to other people if you aren't listening to yourself. Understand fully where you are coming from without judgment (even if it seems unreasonable when you first hear yourself). Have the compassion for your own perspective that you would offer to a friend you love. This is a key step in managing the way you use your power over your employees.

Then, decide deliberately how you want to encounter the responses. There is more information about exactly how to allow and have compassion for the feelings that come up for you regarding the responses, and how to shift those feelings deliberately, in Step 3 of this book. But, the most important thing to remember about this is that your feelings may be valid, reasonable, and fair, but that does not necessarily make them useful for taking your next step.

Just because one feeling is valid does not make other feelings less valid. When you encounter negative responses to a survey, it is fair to feel hurt or even betrayed. Often, we believe our only options are to feel negative "real" feelings or to pretend we feel positive "fake" feelings. That is a false choice because there are hundreds of other feelings that are equally "real" to our negative feelings, but that feel better or are more useful. The options are not limited to "hurt" and "happy," or "betrayed" and "supported," although each of those may be a valid option.

Take some time to allow space for any negative feelings that come up right away when you hear negative feedback, but don't take action from that place. If you are trying to force down how you really feel and pretend you feel positively, this won't work. People can smell it – especially people in a subordinate position to you like employees, students, or even kids. They know when you're covering something up. Once you have taken a little time (which could be one hour, could be one week) to validate and process your feelings away from your employees, you can choose whether to make a shift.

Some information you get may need an immediate response, and so if that is the case, one way to respond and still give yourself space to process is to send out an all-employee email saying something like,

> "I appreciate everyone's participation in the Cultural Health Survey we sent out. I know this can bring up difficult experiences for some, and your willingness to share that and have tough conversations is something I value and admire. Over the next couple of weeks, we will be deciding exactly how to move forward with issues that were raised.
>
> If this survey brought up a problem for you that you feel we should know more about, please talk to a member of the management team you feel comfortable with, and we will include that in our plan moving forward.
>
> If you have a mental or physical condition, and an accommodation would help you perform your job to

the fullest extent, please let us know, and we will start working toward an appropriate accommodation. Thanks again for your participation."

Then, attend to your own experience. If you were giving advice to an employee about how to encounter criticism in her position, what would be your advice about a useful way to encounter it? If you stay in a hurt, defensive place it will shut down your ability to listen and find out the best way to move forward.

The feelings I have found to be incredibly useful to shift to and cultivate for encountering disagreement or negative feedback are openness, curiosity, and courage. Openness acknowledges that you are strong enough to feel negative feelings and still move forward. Curiosity lets you lean in to whatever you are missing and ask more questions. Courage says this is supposed to be scary or painful and it's still worth moving forward. What is a time when you have been incredibly productive in encountering a difficult situation? How did you feel then? That could be a great window into a feeling that works for you for encountering your employees.

After you give your survey, you want to follow up with openness and curiosity to hear about specific problems and how they might be showing up in your workplace. You may want to invite employees to engage in a process to get support and accommodation around their particular issue. You may want to hold open discussions or trainings regarding a problem area. The survey is just a start, and the follow up to the survey makes a huge difference as to whether employees believe you are listening and learn to listen themselves.

These conversations are hard, and they're supposed to be hard. If it is hard, you are doing it right. Also, give yourself the same grace you would give to someone you loved who was going through something hard. Then, after you have awareness over where you are, it's time to start the community healing process.

Takeaways:

- Diagnosing workplace cultural health problems contributes to long-term efficiency because resolving those problems makes employees more productive.
- In order to find out about problems, you have to ask questions that are likely to make it comfortable for an employee to disclose the problems.
- Know what answers you want to find in order to determine what questions to ask.

- Take care of yourself first.
- Listen with curiosity.

Step 2: Confidential Reporting

Chapter 5: Early Reports

"When our local paper picked up the story, social media had a field day. My husband was accused of lying. He was accused of waiting too long to speak up. His deceased mother was accused by members of the church, including the brother (who was a youth pastor at the time the abuse occurred and is now a missionary for the church) of a lead pastor currently working at the church of 'allowing this to happen' by letting her son stay with adult men. I was made out to be a gold digger who encouraged my husband to sue the church because, 'surely we must need the money or use the system.' People I have known for years made comments on the article not knowing it was myself and my husband they were speaking about. People I currently work with made comments not knowing it was me. I can't even imagine how bad it would have been if his name had been attached."
— Anonymous letter from the wife of a survivor

"It took a lot of courage for me to come forward and to work with a therapist to get where I am today. I'm not sure I would have ever come forward without the guarantee that my name wouldn't be made public. It is very painful to look back at my life and see how this has manifested in so many negative ways. If my name were to be public I would have to relive the abuse each and every time I was asked about it."
— Anonymous letter from a survivor

When Naomi was promoted to work in the indoor store of the lumberyard, she was proud. She was good at her job and could run the forklift in the outdoor store as well as anyone, but the indoor store team had benefits she had not previously received. She saw long-time sales people with company cars, company cell phones, and commissions. She worked her way from the accounts receivable job to run the indoor sales. But, as time went on, she did not receive the same benefits as the men who were indoor sales people.

Even worse, when we first met she confessed to me with a great deal of embarrassment that her manager was sexually harassing her. He had pulled up a co-worker's skirt, snapped bras, propositioned Naomi, and showed other invasive offensive behavior. This had been going on in one form or another for eight years. She was terrified because it seemed to have suddenly escalated to him fixating on having a sexual relationship with her. She explained to me that her hair had started falling out and that she would have panic attacks in the parking lot every morning when she drove in for work.

I asked her if she had reported to her company, and she explained that her general manager (the harasser) was who she was supposed to report to. Above him was the regional HR manager. I asked her if she had told the regional HR manager, and this is what she explained:

Months earlier, a man who worked in the outdoor part of the store had called the regional HR manager to complain about this same general manager. He reported that the general manager regularly made discriminatory comments about him and other Latinx workers. So, what did the HR manager do? She knew the general manager, and rather than keep the report confidential and take training and intervention steps to stop the racism, she immediately called the general manager to let him know about the complaint. The general manager retaliated against the outdoor store workers. The discrimination got worse, but the employees were afraid to say anything.

Naomi saw this play out, and she knew it would not be safe to report what was happening with her. She knew the manager had a gun at home, and she was afraid of what he would do to her if she reported. So, in her mind, Naomi was left with the choice to either put herself in physical danger or file a lawsuit and leave the company. She felt she had to choose the latter.

Naomi's story demonstrates the impact it can have not only on individual employees, but also on the business itself, when business owners do not provide employees with a confidential reporting option. In her case, the company lost at least two relatively high-level employees and had the public perception and financial costs of a lawsuit. I represented Naomi to a successful settlement, and as I talked about earlier, Naomi made amazing progress with power dynamics tools. But it's possible that a confidentiality policy and mechanism for responding safely to complaints would have avoided all of those expenses both for Naomi and for her employer.

Now, the counter argument to what I am saying is that when there is a report of misconduct, business owners want to investigate, give each side a fair say, and evaluate what kind of discipline is necessary. I'm not totally discounting that system as necessary if and when discipline is called for and needs to be considered. When an employer finds out about misconduct, it is important to take steps to protect others who might be in danger. And, many employers want to give the accused employees a chance to share their perspective and follow progressive disciplinary standards that create a fair experience for everyone.

If an employer can find out about a problem early on, it is less likely to even require investigation because the problem behavior is often still at a level of interpersonal tension, not disciplinary issues. Also, in most cases that do not involve the government or a union, an accused employee does not have the right to an investigation in an employment situation. Like we talked about before, no complainants want an investigation. They want safety from harassment and fair treatment, so they will tolerate an investigation if necessary. Most harassment, discrimination, and bullying investigations do not result in significant discipline. Those that do result that way generally do so not because of an investigation, but because there is clear evidence at the outset of something that reflects badly on the employer.

Investigations are often a lot of busywork and interviews that are only designed to make it look like employers are doing something about allegations. In reality, they usually result in nothing for the complainant and even less for the accused. If you know an investigation will *not* result in discipline because the accusation does not rise to the level of a disciplinary issue, there are other, better ways to support a complaining employee, which we will talk more about in Step 3.

As a lawyer, I am trained to do investigations, but my experience is that at best they lead to one employee being ostracized from the community – at worst they lead to many employees leaving.

Most Victims Don't Report

The Equal Employment Opportunity Commission (EEOC), which is the federal agency that regulates employment in the United States, reported in a 2016 Task Force Report that roughly three out of four employees experiencing harassment never report the harassment that they experience. Those employees more often leave their jobs rather than face the potential retaliation, ridicule, questioning, blame, or even silence that most complainants face. The task force report describes that the most common response to a report of harassment is retaliation.

Because women, minorities, and other disadvantaged groups are most likely to face harassment, this has created a category of "career refugees" escaping from one job to another because they are targeted based on characteristics they have no power to change. Employees who have done nothing wrong are bearing the financial burden of harassment.

Employers, too, face the expense of retraining, and the EEOC alone reports that it recovered $164.5 million from employers on behalf of employees in 2015 (in 2018, the EEOC reported it recovered $70 million from employers based on sexual harassment claims alone). Those millions are only the "tip of the iceberg" when it comes to the investments business owners are making into ignoring and fostering harassing and discriminatory workplaces.

The only people even close to benefiting from this tremendous investment into a culture of silence are the worst of the worst – the people who intentionally want to harass and discriminate against others. I have seen rare instances of those employees, but the majority of actual harassers and people who discriminate, in my experience, have simply not received appropriate information, training, and consequences around discriminatory behavior. They have been surrounded by people who believe the same things as them, and so they have not had their biases seriously challenged or really considered the impact of their behavior.

Most people who harass are actually "good" people in other areas. They are engaging in problem behavior, though, and that problem behavior can even become dangerous. When that problem behavior is never spoken about, they have no chance to change, but they will keep driving away good employees and interfering with workplace productivity.

Beyond merely interfering with productivity, a culture of shaming and job insecurity can actually contribute to harassment and discrimination. Research out of Ohio University conducted by Leah Halper and Kimberly Rios in 2018, for example, asked men to answer questions around sexual harassment. They were asked to imagine themselves in a powerful employment position over a female employee and to indicate whether they would ask for sexual favors in exchange for job-related benefits. The respondents then answered questions about their own self-esteem and how important they perceived other people's opinion. The study concluded that fear that others would perceive them as incompetent was a predictor of whether a man would sexually harass.

So, job and interpersonal security can be an indicator of whether a workplace will become harassing or discriminatory. Despite the evidence that job security contributes to workplace cultural health, if you are not focused on that goal, there is often the fallback option of disciplining employees for any allegation of misconduct – but only if you find out about it.

If you don't know about the problem, you can't intervene. But, you are unlikely to learn about the problem unless you put into place procedures to protect the employees who are willing to report, such as designated confidential reporting procedures for reports of problems that do not rise to the level of physical danger. For example, giving employees access to multiple reporting options like a manager, human resources person or other administrative staff, *and* an outside reporting person can allow them to choose a comfortable reporting person. In communicating a problem with a comfortable reporting person, the employee is also more likely to feel able to make clear choices about the type of response they want.

It is important to have employees designated as reporting options trained as to how to respond, however, because many managers falsely perceive a complaining employee wants confidentiality where she doesn't or vice versa. Employees are also likely to perceive reporting people as encouraging them to do the opposite of what they want (for example, a complainant who wants confidentiality is likely to perceive a reporting person as discouraging it and someone who wants an investigation is likely to also perceive discouragement that way.) This typically stems from the employee's own self-doubt and criticism, and it is an important component to hold space for but create clarity around.

To the extent possible, designated confidential reporting people should be trained to give options and to be guided by the complaining employee's genuine preference, without encouraging the employee one way or another. If the complaining employee wants to resolve the problem while maintaining confidentiality and just needs some advice, the designated reporting person should still make sure to check in about the problem later. If the complaining employee wants someone else to lead the response to the problem, it is important that she understand clearly how the non-confidential process will go. (Chapter 6 talks more about how to decide when investigations are necessary and Chapter 9 talks more about creating transparent processes.)

The Reality of Retaliation

When I ask employees why they want to report harassment or pursue lawsuits against their employers for discrimination, the most common response I hear is, "I don't want this to happen to someone else." Employees who report feel tremendous responsibility to protect other people like them from experiencing the burden and stress of abuse.

But, when faced with the reality of how much worse things could get if they stand up publicly against a harasser and an employer who both seem so much more powerful than them, many employees reasonably are not willing to sacrifice their own safety for the mere possibility that it might protect their community.

Within the law, there are some protections for people who are willing to come forward to report crimes that are considered stigmatizing like those involving sexual misconduct. For example, the adults who reported being molested as children by predators in organizations like the Catholic Church and the Boy Scouts of America were able to do so because they could file cases under pseudonyms like "John Doe" and "Jane Doe." Many have been too afraid of retaliation against themselves and their families to use their legal names, and would otherwise have decided not to go forward with cases that have created more safety in our communities. When someone is the victim of a sexual crime, and they are forced to have their name associated with it, often the community perceives there is something wrong with that person, even though, in fact, they did nothing wrong. This is particularly true in small communities, and no matter how large a company is, most work communities feel small.

A man I worked with was a millwright in a small logging community, for example. When he was a child, his brother was arrested and prosecuted for sexually molesting him. This man had recovered from the experience until, as an adult who was married to a woman and had two children, the other men he worked with found out about his experience and started taunting and bullying him with gay slurs. Their perception was that gay people are perpetrators of sexual crimes and somehow he had become a perpetrator of sexual crimes because he had experienced a crime. The harassment became so cruel that he went on medication and ultimately felt he had no choice but to move away from the community.

Recently, I had the chance to work on a protection in Oregon legal rules for victims coming forward in civil court. Traditionally, victims had been allowed to ask in court to use pseudonyms like "Jane Doe" to protect their names in public documents up to the time of trial. But a retired judge began advocating in 2017 to take away this opportunity to ask for a pseudonym. Because of some hard work on the part of a committee of advocates and other judges that I was able to be a part of, a rule was passed allowing victims to continue to ask for protection. The quotes I included at the beginning of this chapter were submitted in support of this rule change.

In the final meeting to vote on the rule, Brenda Tracy, a survivor advocate, who speaks about her experience of rape at Oregon State University in order to advocate for other survivors, gave a very powerful speech about her experiences. She said that she, like other survivors who have come out, receives harassing social media posts, bullying letters, and even death threats almost daily. She said that it is not everyone who is strong enough to continue speaking about their experience after they receive so much hatred, but it is worth it to her. The real, present statement of someone who experiences this kind of retaliation was very powerful in demonstrating how confidentiality can determine whether a community hears about a crime or whether it stays secret.

It is no different, though it is sometimes even worse, in a job than in a school or religious community. When an employee feels targeted or unsafe, fear of losing her job or losing her professional community can be a huge deterrent from reporting. When employees do report, they often are so sensitive to retaliation that they may perceive it even when it is not intended. But, more commonly, employers and co-workers who know about the problem often try to avoid the employee, either so as not to cause more problems, or because they actually don't like the report and believe there is something wrong with the employee.

This is similar to what happens with death and grief. When a family member dies, people often report intense loneliness and that their friends and family start avoiding them. Most friends would never intentionally avoid someone suffering (nor would most managers or co-workers for that matter), but we often worry that we will do something to make things worse, so we try to avoid things altogether. Unfortunately, this often makes things worse. Even worse, there are also those who avoid grieving people because they actually believe there is something wrong with the grieving process, too.

Ostracizing, avoiding, and leaving employees alone can feel like retaliation, regardless of the motivation for it. After all, it is not how we typically respond when an employee accomplishes something huge in her position. For an employee who has made an accomplishment, we surround her with praise and give her more attention. And, reporting harassment and discrimination is a huge, courageous accomplishment. Seventy-five percent of employees are too afraid to try.

Navigating Confidentiality

Some employees do not want their reports to be confidential. Others do. The best way to navigate that is to make no assumption about what the employee wants and to ask questions. A question like, "Have you thought about whether you would be comfortable with me talking to the other person about this problem?" feels more neutral than a question like, "Do you want to remain anonymous?"

It is pretty common for employees to feel pressured, whether you suggest that their report stay confidential or whether you suggest that it become public. Regardless of what you think is best, your opinion matters. Your obligation as an employer to keep a safe workspace is *your* obligation, independent of what the employee wants. But you can still work with the reporting employee in a productive way, even if you feel you have an obligation to confront the behavior. Sometimes, you can suggest that you feel you need to confront the behavior and ask the employee if she has any preferences or concerns about that. Other times, all the employee needs is permission, perspective, and advice about how to handle a problem situation. Most employees are willing to allow their report to become known if it is done in a respectful way.

In addition to a survey, this is another opportunity to listen openly to the employee's experience and preferences, assuming that even if you don't understand, you can ask enough questions to really see the validity of her perspective. It is hard to listen to employee complaints, and it is hard for employees to complain. Often both employers and employees engage in sugar-coating, a form of people pleasing that will not allow any discussion of real problems. The employer expects the employee to maintain a "positive attitude" and the employee wants to please the employer and prove she's a smart, tough worker.

But people pleasing is really lying. It doesn't work and it's like putting glitter onto a gaping wound. There's no healing, just cover up. Most employers do not want to cultivate a manipulative, deceitful workforce, but that is exactly what they do when they are not able to hold space for discussion of real problems. If you are going to truly lead your employees in an inclusive way, you have to do your work first to see your own biases and taboo topics. You have to be willing to do your own work on power dynamics and step into a place where you are powerful enough to talk about hard things. You have to be willing to be uncomfortable.

You have the opportunity to be a safe space for employees to come and learn how to lead and grow in their own power. Many people see themselves as too fragile to hear complaints or deal with conflict, but no one actually is that fragile.

Most employees who have the opportunity to maintain confidentiality come to realize that they are strong enough to go forward without it. But, when they are not given that option, they are likely to avoid reporting anything until it has gotten so bad that they are ready to quit. If you are able to do the hard work first of looking at your own biases, stepping into your power, and creating a safe space to talk about difficult things, you are more likely to hear about problems before it's too late.

Takeaways:

- Fear of retaliation prevents the majority of employees experiencing problems from coming forward.
- The majority of employees who report problems experience retaliation.
- The availability of a confidential reporting option, such as designating particular reporting options inside and outside of your company, allows an

employee to report and get help without the fear of retaliation.

- With a confidentiality option available and respectful disclosure of the report, many employees are willing to support the efforts an employer needs to take to keep the company safe.

Chapter 6: Investigations

"Then he asked me if I wanted to 'pursue a formal investigation,'" Maia told me about her conversation with an administrator where she worked. "I didn't know what that meant," she said, "so I tried to ask him about the process. "Does that mean the harasser will get notice that I reported?' I asked him. And he accused me of being vindictive! I started crying while I was talking to him and he could tell how much stress I was under. All I wanted to do was keep my job and get some protection! I didn't know what it meant to have a formal or informal investigation. I didn't want an investigation at all! I just wanted to get away from the harasser. I asked if the harasser would find out because I wanted to make sure I was out of the department so he couldn't hurt me anymore before he found out. Vindictive? I put up with this behavior for four years! I was never vindictive! I probably wasn't vindictive enough."

Maia is one of many employees who has explained to me the problems with the investigation model of responding to employee complaints. The question is, once you've heard from an employee, how do you want to respond to the report? What is the immediate action you want to have available in your toolbox if you get a report you are not prepared for? My view is that it does not have to be complicated, but you should be prepared both with support for the complainant and for protections around the problem employee. An investigation is a completely separate consideration.

If you go forward with an investigation, it is unlikely that the complaining employee can truly maintain confidentiality, and so that is something to navigate respectfully with the complaining employee. If that employee will not cooperate, your investigation will be severely limited and possibly unsuccessful, so there is an advantage to working with the complaining employee instead of against her.

One point of confusion most employees have, when an employer immediately encounters a report with an offer of investigation rather than support, is that they often do not encounter an investigation model of response until they are reporting something like harassment, discrimination, or retaliation, even though they report other problems. For example, picture this scenario:

You're an employee and you work for a company for a couple of years. Then one day, your sandwich is stolen out of the employee refrigerator. You go to the human resources person and let them know what happened. The human resources representative says, "I'm so sorry that happened. That's not okay. I will send out an email letting everyone know someone's food was taken and reminding them to be careful and respectful about other people's food or we will all start having tighter restrictions. Anything else I can do? Can I order you in a lunch?"

Work continues with no more sandwich stealing.

A year later, someone deletes one of your files in a shared folder. You are livid because you worked on that file for weeks. You go to your supervisor and let her know what happened. She immediately gets on the phone to IT to try to see what she can do to recover your file. She too sympathizes and clearly understands how frustrating it is to work that long and have the work disappear. "Is there any chance you emailed it to someone so there is a copy?" She emails the department with a reminder to never delete files from the shared folder without approval.

Shortly after that, someone new starts working for the company, and he makes you very uncomfortable. He comments on your clothing often and one time he makes a gesture like he is cupping breasts and winks at you. He asks you if you have a boyfriend. Then, you decide to work late one night, and he suddenly is at your desk, even though you thought you were alone. He doesn't hurt you, but just the fact that he is there sends you into a panic. You wait and wait, but after months, you decide to sit down with your supervisor and HR representative and confess to them how afraid you feel. They say in unison, "Do you want us to conduct an investigation?"

You are confused and feel somewhat defensive, but you're not sure why. You already felt ashamed and embarrassed to be talking to your bosses about being sexualized by a colleague. But now you think, "Am I wrong? Why do they need to investigate? Is it just because they think I'm not telling the truth about this?" You wonder, "They didn't suggest investigating whether I really had a sandwich. Why investigate whether I'm telling the truth about this? What does it mean to conduct an investigation? Does it mean they think I'm a liar?"

Now, there is some strong evidence that when people who have a disadvantaged characteristic (female, non-Christian, non-white, differently abled, non-straight, transgender, etc.) report harassment or discrimination, our natural inclination is not to believe them. And when I say "our" I don't mean people with advantaged characteristics. I mean everyone, including others with disadvantaged characteristics. One reason is that we unconsciously believe that if we acknowledge discrimination and other wrongs exist, then it opens up the possibility that they could happen to us. If our unconscious brain rejects that they exist or justifies them, it feels safer. This process usually happens so unconsciously and so quickly that we only register it as slight unease. We have the thought, "That couldn't be true," for a split second. But then we want to be fair, so we offer to investigate whether it's true or not.

The complaining employee *knows* it's true. She doesn't want an investigation to find out if it's true. Like with getting her sandwich stolen, she just wants the behavior to be corrected.

Worse than the natural, unconscious inclination to deny discrimination exists because of the mistaken idea it could hurt us to acknowledge it, some employers deliberately want to initiate investigations to cover up conduct they know is happening because they believe exposing it will cost them money. They have no thought about their company's cultural health experience or their employees' safety, but they see the accusation itself (rather than the discrimination) as a potential financial cost. This is just incredibly short-sighted and is the equivalent of deliberately investing in harassment and discrimination as a company policy.

Because you are reading this book, I imagine that is not your perspective and that you are interested in actually creating an inclusive company culture, with all of the dynamics and communication hurdles that involves. You probably know that having a diverse, inclusive workplace will actually make it more successful and efficient in the long run. It doesn't necessarily make it easy in the short-run, though. If you have a friend who falls more on the side of using investigations to cover up bad conduct, that is a brilliant friend to use to practice the power dynamics master skills I'm going to teach you in Step 3. I know it might sound outrageous, but here are *legitimately good reasons* that your friend wants to cover up bad conduct. In her mind, it is probably related to loyalty, forgiveness, privacy, and individualized values. Each of these has nothing actually wrong with it. But, fostering harassment and discrimination is never, in my experience, a good way to honor those values. It is simply a thinking error, and it may even be a thinking error that your friend feels she has benefited from.

When Investigations Are Necessary

Investigations are often not necessary in response to harassment and discrimination allegations. But the way you know if they are necessary is by looking at other times when you would normally conduct an investigation. An investigation is a mechanism to protect an accused employee from being unfairly disciplined or fired. It is not a mechanism to protect a complaining employee. Most states have "at-will" employment status, meaning an employer could fire an employee for any reason, unless it is specifically prohibited by law.

If a long-time client of a company complains that a staff person was threatening, for example, often an employer will immediately suspend or fire the staff person without any kind of investigation. The *allegation alone* is enough to trigger the discipline. The employer may give the employee an opportunity to prove themselves, but the employer will likely not force the client to prove the employee did something wrong.

This is because in the United States, as we have established the law now, there is no right to have a job. A job is something we prove we are capable of doing well, and then we have the privilege of continuing to keep it. That is not necessarily the best way to manage employment structure, and many employers want to provide greater protections for employees for good reason. Unions have also done a lot to give employees better rights and more protections. Increasing job security is a crucial step to reducing harassment and discrimination because, as we talked about previously, insecurity in a job position is likely the number one indicator of whether a man will sexually harass, for example. When employees are afraid of being fired or laid off, discrimination, harassment, abuse, and bullying increase.

As a legal matter, it is important to know that it is illegal to retaliate against an employee because that employee reports harassment or discrimination, and there are other areas where it is illegal to retaliate against or fire an employee (if you want more information about that, it is important to talk with an attorney in your state about your individual situation). It is not illegal to discipline an employee because of an allegation of harassment or discrimination, any more than it would be illegal to discipline an employee for an allegation of theft or rudeness to a client. Employees who are accused of harassment or discrimination do not receive special protections simply because the allegation relates to harassment or discrimination. Government employees and unionized employees have a higher level of protection than this, but it is the general rule.

In many companies there is conduct that is tolerated zero times and *even an allegation* of that conduct triggers discipline. This is because the reputation of engaging in that conduct is so contrary to the values of your business that it is harmful. It could cost licensing or shut down the business. What is that conduct in your business?

Once you have a list of what that conduct is in your business, it should be evenly applied, no matter who the accuser or the respondent is.

You may be asking, "Don't false allegations happen all the time? How can I have a universal zero tolerance policy when I know people make things up?" False accusations *do happen*. They happen for every type of misconduct at about the same rate, according to research studies. There is estimated to be about a two to ten percent rate of false reporting for every type of crime. Much larger is the percentage of unreported misconduct (about seventy-five percent). It is true that if you have zero tolerance for conduct, even allegations of conduct, a false allegation could do damage. It is statistically more likely, though, that if there is an allegation, there are four other unreported incidents of the same conduct.

You may choose not to have zero-tolerance behavior, and that is your choice as a business owner. For some companies and industries it makes more sense to have zero-tolerance behavior than others, and so without knowing the work you do, I can't have an opinion on it. Creating an inclusive workplace is not about forcing a culture of fake tolerance where no one faces consequences. It is about serving the mission of your company by identifying and openly solving problems. Creating consequences for unacceptable behavior is part of creating an inclusive workplace. You and the people you work with have key insight into what is unacceptable in your workplace. I will say that my opinion in general is that there is always room for correction, reform, forgiveness, and change. For some industries, based on regulations or standards, that is not realistic, though. As with some of the other steps in this book, I have seen business owners struggle with setting clear expectations, and I encourage you to have someone outside of your business help you if this part of the process seems easier said than done.

After you have listed the zero-tolerance conduct, the next step is making a clear list of offenses that could result in separating an employee from the company. If you want lists of some types of conduct that you might want to include, you can look to professional standards of conduct for your industry or even the criminal law in your state.

Do you want discriminatory behavior to be included in that list? If so, do you want words alone to be enough? How severe or pervasive does the language need to be? Does one incident of discriminatory words count as enough to qualify for termination of employment? What if the discriminatory behavior comes from someone in a disadvantaged group (for example, what if a black woman calls a white man in a superior position a "cracker" in a joking tone?). What if she didn't mean any harm and is very regretful when she finds out it was hurtful? Would you apply that standard equally if the white man made a derogatory comment to the black woman and was regretful about it? There are reasons to make more room and allowances for groups with historically disadvantaged characteristics than those with traditionally advantaged characteristics, and so what I am offering is that deciding your policy (whatever it is) ahead of time, and knowing why you have that policy, will help you evenly apply it.

Discrimination comes in many, many forms, and most of them are invisible. Discrimination includes both punching some-one in the face because they have a characteristic that's different than yours and not hiring them because there's "just something that doesn't resonate" with you. It includes both making vulgar jokes that demean another person because of something they can't change about themselves and it can include talking over them in meetings because in your view they're not asserting them-selves enough.

Harassment, too, comes in many forms, and some are invisible. Harassment can include physical violence and death threats. It can also include subtle, persistent, invasive attention and touching that doesn't leave bruises.

My point is that if you hold an "investigation" and you determine that the conduct *did* happen, what are you going to do about it? If, like with the missing sandwiches and the missing file, it is going to result in a training and a reminder on profession-alism standards for the entire staff, why are you waiting for an in-vestigation to do that? If it is going to result in safety protections around the alleged offender for client-safety reasons, why are you going to wait for an investigation to do that? If it is going to result in power-dynamics support for the complainant, why are you go-ing to wait for an investigation to do that? Is an investigation go-ing to convince you that staff does not need retraining, client safety isn't an issue, and the complaining employee doesn't need support? That seems unlikely.

Often an investigation has an unclear result that looks something like, both parties seem to be telling the truth from their perspective and they have very different perspectives. "He thought he was encouraging her"; "She thought he was talking to her like she was a child because she's a younger woman." Both could be true at the same time. Is investigating going to help you decide how to intervene in that situation?

Ask yourself how an investigation will help you deal with this in an active, helpful way, not just help with ignoring the conflict. If you ignore it, it will definitely get worse one way or another – usually "worse" looks like losing employees, sometimes it looks like getting sued.

After you have addressed the immediate steps you can take without an investigation, *that* is the time to decide whether an investigation is necessary. After you have sent a reminder to staff about professionalism and respect; provided support, permissions, and training to the complainant; and created any necessary safety protections around the problem employee, you may decide that you may need to build evidence in order to fire the problem employee for cause. In that case an investigation may help you and not be so offensive to the complainant.

Who Is Right?

I was giving a presentation to a group of lawyers about what I teach, and a very angry gentleman raised his hand and asked, exasperated, "But how does this help me know who is telling the truth?!" If your mission is to make your best evidence-based evaluation of who is telling the truth and what "really" happened, an investigation is necessary, and the traditional tools of evidence-gathering and witness interviews are what you should use. You could even take a course in identifying truthful and lying indicators or hire a polygraph expert. Sometimes, at the end of an investigation, it is possible to feel reasonably confident about what happened. Almost always, though, our own perspective about what happened is influenced by our biases. Each witness's statement is influenced by that person's bias. No replication or investigation fact-finding of "what happened" will exactly mirror what actually happened. We see this in the criminal law where, despite the highest level of protection for defendants, people are still wrongly convicted. If I discover the simple solution to investigations and knowing who to believe, I will let you know.

Sometimes, we *really don't believe a person*, but it's because of who that person is, not what that person is saying. The problem is that people who are unreliable in general are also targets for abuse. While I was in school, for example, a classmate accused another classmate of rape. The woman who made the accusation was someone many believed to be at least an incredibly unreliable person, but at worst a pathological liar. Pretty soon though, after her allegation, three more women came forward reporting the same experience with the accused rapist. It became clear that the man who was accused was targeting vulnerable women and drugging them. But some continued to disbelieve one or another of the woman *because of her vulnerable characteristic.* In this case, the vulnerable characteristic was that she was an unreliable person in other situations. Vulnerable characteristics, even unreliability in one area, do not immediately indicate a lie when it comes to misconduct allegations.

Sometimes, we *really don't believe something happened* because it sounds too horrible to think someone we know would do that. When I was working on the resolution process for Rhea's employees in the case I talked about at the beginning of this book, the woman accused of harassment was genuinely devastated at the allegation, and I sat with her for about four hours while she cried. She vehemently denied that the man could have experienced anything with her that he could think was harassment or assault. She explained to me that she believed that anyone accused of sexual assault was scum, so she now had to believe she was scum. Once she learned about the specifics of the allegations though, she said she could understand how the man could have had a different perspective than she did, and she still knew she would never have intentionally hurt him. She shifted from vehement denial to more understanding and compassion. Her vision of what he was alleging was, to her, unacceptable from any human. Once she shifted her understanding though, she could see two different, valid perspectives.

When we *really don't believe* someone, sometimes we are right and should listen to our intuition. More often, though, it is because of our own unconscious bias. It is because of the movie we are playing in our head about who the accuser is or what the allegations might mean.

Those are opportunities for every business owner to have compassion for herself, and also for her to questions what biases might be lurking in her brain that might not be serving her.

The power dynamic model of response, versus the investigation model of response, *does* help employers get a clearer picture of what happened. This is because when employees can manage their thinking, feelings, and how they engage with power dynamics, they are better at truthfully telling stories and presenting evidence. They tell a clearer story – whether it is a complaining employee or a responding employee.

But understand *why* you want to know who is right. Some responses need to be automatic when an employee complains. That employee needs support, permission to take care of herself, and even training on how to do that. Depending on the alleged conduct, it's possible that an investigation is not even necessary because a reminder about professional conduct or all-staff training could be enough to correct the problem behavior. Or the allegation could be so severe that an allegation alone is enough to separate the employee. In the event an investigation is necessary, remember it is not what is going to solve the situation for the complainant. Any punishment for the responding employee is not going to solve things for the complaining employee. An investigation *might* serve you, and there is nothing wrong with that. It is not a catch-all solution to workplace cultural health problems.

Takeaways:

- No employees who complain about problem behavior at work do so because they want an investigation – they want safety, support, and permission to take care of themselves.
- An investigation is sometimes necessary to provide the accused employee protections around whether discipline is fair.
- Determine ahead of time what behaviors require an investigation to protect the accused employee, what behaviors are zero-times events, and what behaviors require retraining and support but will not ultimately lead to discipline.
- Do your work first. Understand your own bias or bring someone in who is less likely to have those biases.

Step 3: Power Dynamics Model

Chapter 7: Power Dynamics at Work

"Defense is the first act of war."

– Byron Katie

When Firing Isn't Enough

Iris was crying as she told me, "They fired him, and they acted like that solved the problem. I know they think it did, but for me that was just one of the problems. I'm the *only woman* working in a group of all men and they're all ten to twenty years older than me. I've gotten no support. I called attorney offices when it was happening and no one would help me." Iris had "successfully" reported harassment, meaning her employer believed her because she had proof in text messages of what she was experiencing, and they fired the harasser. But, for Iris, firing him had almost nothing to do with creating safety for her at work or helping her. She wanted to learn how to have a safe, fair work experience. She wanted to feel supported by her employer.

Firing her harasser had nothing to do with what she wanted. It wasn't bad, but it didn't address or even acknowledge her experience.

This goes again to the fact that an investigation and an investigation outcome is about the problem employee and the employer, not the employee who reported the problem. The employee who reported almost always needs support too, and probably does not even know what that should look like.

In many situations, employees who report harassment are not even as lucky as Iris, and they face blame and retaliation from their employers. In order to look at the underlying causes of toxic behavior at work and truly address them, we have to consider two different problems at work, like we did in the last chapter, and consider why we treat them so differently.

Imagine you have a co-worker who keeps stealing your pens. Most of us have had something like that happen – a co-worker who takes the hole punch to her desk every time she needs to use it and doesn't return it, or one who takes your pen every time she comes by your desk. Most of us would have no problem with asking the pen-stealing co-worker to stop. We would not feel shame in confronting her about it or even in going to her desk and taking the pens back. We mark our pens with tape or tie plastic flowers to them because we expect pen stealing culprits to exist. If an employee came to you as a boss and told you that she wanted you to get the pens back for her, you might think it was a little bit shy that she didn't want to get the pens herself, but you probably wouldn't think she was a liar because of it.

So, why is harassment and discrimination *such a different experience*? Why do we respond completely differently to harassment, discrimination, bullying, and other toxic behaviors at work than we do to pen stealing?

The first answer you might want to give is that harassment, discrimination, bullying, and other toxic behaviors are more serious than pen stealing, and so we should act differently. That is a totally fair answer, but I would say that if something is more serious, we should respond more effectively, not less effectively, to the problem. We should take the skills we already have with pen-stealing and enhance them, not throw them out the window. And that is not the case if you compare those two problems. If the seriousness of the issue were the difference, we should be responding at least as effectively to abuse as we do to pen stealing.

Harassment: Power or Sex?

I believe the real answer is that a complaint about abusive behavior at work speaks to an underlying cultural health issue in the workplace in the way that pen stealing does not. It speaks to an imbalance of power that we are still learning to navigate in culture.

Now, in the past, there has been a debate about whether sexual harassment, for example, is about sex or power. The traditional feminist analysis has always been that abusive behavior is about power, not about sexual attraction. Others have argued, though, that sometimes there is just a clumsy person who is not good at flirting and becomes harassing because of his awkwardness. In that case, the harassment could be about sexual attraction, not about power.

The problem with both analyses is that they both have tended to speak to the perpetrator's perspective and tried to understand why the perpetrator is behaving in a harassing way. Is he just awkward and attracted to his target, or is he trying to keep her fearful and powerless?

From the targeted person's perspective, harassment and discrimination are *always* about power.

Anne Clark described this perfectly in her blog post, *The Rock Test: A Hack for Men Who Don't Want to Be Accused of Harassment*. In the post, she quotes a *New York Times* article saying that men are becoming hyperaware of their interactions with women and avoiding women at work altogether. Clark explains that navigating how to interact with women at work is simple. She says, "It's as clear cut as this: Treat all women like you would treat Dwayne 'The Rock' Johnson." She recommends that when men are working with a co-worker, and it turns out she's pretty "in the face, even," so things become confusing, all you have to do is close your eyes and picture Dwayne "The Rock" Johnson instead.

Then, when you're picturing someone who could crush your skull with his bare hands, it becomes clear how to behave. The Rock Test perfectly shows how important power dynamics are in workplace abuse situations.

Still, The Rock Test continues to speak to the perpetrator's perspective, as we have done for decades, to try to get workplace abusers to stop abusing their power (or stop inappropriately pursuing sexual attraction, depending on the perpetrator's perspective of problem).

I hate to break it to you, but trying to get harassers to stop harassing has not worked yet. With about seventy-five percent of harassment incidents unreported, one in five women becoming career refugees because of harassment (and unknown statistics related to other disadvantaged career refugee groups), and seventy-five percent of reporters facing retaliation, there is a lot of work left to do. You probably already knew that and have had your own experience with the ineffectiveness of this broken system. But without something that actually does work to replace it, it's hard for business owners and workplace leaders to know what to do. At least teaching people what harassment and discrimination are is something, right?

One of the reasons it is not working to focus on the harasser's perspective in trying to stop harassment is that we're trying to get people to change when they have no motivation to change. When the targeted employees are leaving careers and experiencing retaliation, the perpetrators are actually getting rewarded for their harassing behavior.

Cognitive Bias and Power Dynamics

The traditional policies, trainings, and interventions around abuse at work try to help potential perpetrators understand what harassment and discrimination are so that they don't get fired for it. If you think about it, this makes sense for a lot of reasons: If perpetrators stopped harassing, the rest of us wouldn't have to worry about our safety. Also, the criminal justice system, which most other systems have been taught to imitate, is intentionally focused on protecting the civilian population from an oppressive government. So, in the criminal justice system, we worry the most about preventing someone from being wrongly sent to prison. In the employment system, much of what we do wrongly mimics this model, so we worry about someone being wrongly fired by an oppressive boss. We don't do this consistently, though, and so the random application of criminal law standards creates more chaos.

The trouble with both models, and why they have been ineffective, is that simply putting someone in prison or firing someone does not address the root cause of either the problem of crime or the problem of toxic behavior at work. We have tried for centuries to put the "bad people" on an island so that we don't have to deal with them, and it's unlikely to start magically working now. I call it the "hunt for the bad apple." We want to find the bad apple in the bunch and cut off the "bad" part or toss out the apple, and by doing so protect the rest of the apples in the basket. Sadly, we are not apples. The longer we hunt for the bad ones, the more focused we become on fear of the rotten.

Even sadder, all of our brains have the biases that create discriminatory and harassing behavior. We may see one person behave in a way that we consider to be outside of the bounds of what is acceptable or appropriate, but when it comes to abuse at work, what we see is almost always only the tip of the iceberg. More than that, if the abuse does not get stopped immediately or we struggle with how to stop it, it is usually a sign of an underlying systemic support of the abuse. "Underlying systemic support" happens when people in higher positions in a business have an unconscious assumption something is normal.

What I'm trying to say is that all of us have discrimination in our own brains. The research on brains calls this "cognitive bias," and often it just looks like trusting the people we know more than the people we don't know. It looks like seeing someone do one good thing and believing they are a "good person."

Or, it looks like seeing someone do one bad thing, and being unable to acknowledge it because we've seen good things from them in the past. The reality is that people we don't know are trustworthy at the same rate as people we know, possibly more or less, but always unrelated to whether we know them or not. People who do "good" things also do bad things.

This kind of cognitive bias expands to believing that people who are like us are good people and people who are unlike us are bad people. The people who like our favorite sports team are better than the people who like competitive teams, for example. It makes sense that our brains have evolved to believe our tribe is better than the other tribes. This kind of loyalty creates strong bonds and safety.

It also creates discrimination. It plants in our minds the idea that people who do not look like us are bad at the skills we care about because of characteristics that are unrelated to the skill. For example, it makes as much sense to say that people who like yellow shirts are bad at math as to say women are bad at math. It makes as much sense to say people who drive blue cars are good leaders as to say that white people are good leaders. The characteristics are unrelated to the skill, and pairing them creates a false correlation. Some people who are female, non-white, wear yellow shirts, and drive non-blue cars are probably good at math and good leaders.

But each of our brains creates these correlations in order to make our thought processing run faster. And our unconscious brains are incredibly good at running efficiently. Stopping to consider whether blue cars are really related to leadership interferes with our brain grouping things together in order to create more efficiency. So, when we have the privilege of ignoring these false correlations, our brains go happily along ignoring them.

People who benefit (even unintentionally) from discrimination have to fight with our unconscious brains, which only want to run efficiently, in order to consider and shift the thinking errors that create discrimination. If you know a white woman who brags that she "doesn't see color," this is an example of that kind of discrimination. She has the unconscious privilege of not seeing color because she has the culturally-favored characteristic of being white. This creates a bias, which inevitably results in discriminatory use of that privilege.

That means that it is much more difficult for those of us who have benefitted from discrimination and harassment to make any kind of shift. Harassers are strongly motivated by their unconscious brains not to see what they're doing as harassment. The social stigma around harassment and discrimination creates even more external motivation for each of us to ignore and repress any thoughts we might have that are discriminatory. When we ignore and repress them, they don't go away, they become assumptions. The more we don't want to look at them, the more they become implanted as biased beliefs. This means that when white women who have experienced sexism are repressing their own biases rather than questioning them, we have a difficult time seeing bias we might have around race. Black women who have full physical abilities, but who feel like it's unacceptable to acknowledge their brains might have biases, will have a difficult time seeing bias they might have around disability. Each of us has areas of privilege and areas of disadvantage. Where we have privilege, our brains want to protect us from seeing that the disadvantage other people have in that area might be because of discrimination. Recognizing discrimination and questioning our bias slows things down in a way our unconscious brains hate.

Training perpetrators not to harass is unlikely to stop harassment and discrimination … ever. It is at least the slowest way to stop discrimination. Instead, when each of us can openly talk about the biases we engage in and that we see around us, we can create a shift without waiting for people who do not have our unique viewpoints on where biases exist. People who can't see it can't change it, so we can't wait for them.

The other reason it is important to empower the employees who see the discrimination, rather than expecting those perpetrating discrimination to change first, is that what one person believes is harassment or discrimination is often different than what another person believes is harassment or discrimination. I have been in a situation where someone told a hilarious joke about me being murdered by a serial rapist that made me genuinely laugh until I cried (true fact). But I have also been in a different situation where someone touched my shoulder and I went into a panic. Some people would have been reasonably offended by the murder joke and not offended by the shoulder rub. Individually, many of us have different expectations of what behavior we want to tolerate and what behavior we do not want to tolerate.

Some one-size-fits-all rules can work. For example, in the sample employee handbook I offer at ErisResolution.com/handbook, I encourage employers to set the rule that touching is not expected at work and that any touching requires active consent ahead of time. This is because for employees who have experienced physical abuse or intimidation in the past, touching at work is often an unnecessary and easily avoided trigger. Often in smaller, family-run companies implementing this kind of rule can be tough, though, because there is a family culture of being "huggers." The trouble is that any culture that routinely invades the personal space of a member is vulnerable to abuses. Where we can implement rules that expect everyone to be cautious of invading anyone else's space, exceptions are still possible, and an active-consent "hugger" culture just makes sure everyone is into it, not only those in positions of power.

Managing Power Dynamics at Work

So, what does work? In my experience, in order to effectively stop abuse at work, we have to support both the victim and the perpetrator in understanding and appropriately using power dynamics.

Most of us spend our days at work feeling like this:

(Everyone Else)   (Me)

Often perpetrators feel this way even more than victims of harassment. Those who feel powerless are much more likely to perpetrate abuse than those who understand the power they have. This is because we justify exaggerated and abusive behavior when we are "defending ourselves." Like we talked about before, the research shows that men are more likely to perpetrate harassment if they feel insecure in their jobs, for example. The cliché for this is the "pecking order," referring to the hierarchy by which chickens abuse each other. The chicken with the most status pecks at the chicken with the next most status, and down the chain. The classic description of this with humans is the boss abuses the employee, who abuses his wife, who abuses their child, who is a bully at school.

We end up like this:

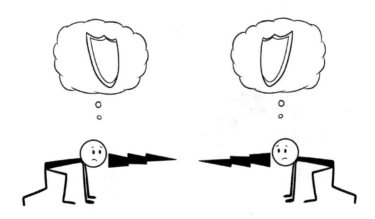

I hope we can all agree that it's time to be better than chickens.

The only way I have found to really understand and shift power dynamics in each of our individual situations is to understand the root cause of power and powerlessness.

It may sound trite, but the root cause of power and powerlessness is not government systems or cultural training, it is our thoughts. The good news about this is that if we needed to wait for government systems and culture to change in order to shift power dynamics, we would probably be screwed. Those structures shift at such a slow pace that waiting for them may help future generations, but it will not help you create a healthy, safe workplace culture right now.

We often identify so strongly with our thoughts, believing they are observations, that we make assumptions about our powerlessness that are not correct.

In reality, all of us have the same amount of time as Beyoncé and Elon Musk, and our personal power is no different. We may be raised with assumptions about our personal power, like our time, but just because we believe something does not make it true.

There is always an objective reality to any situation, and that reality is always neutral. Everyone can agree on it.

Each of us has a thought about that objective reality.

Our thoughts create our feelings.

Our feelings motivate what we do or don't do in response to the neutral reality.

What we do or don't do determines the impact we make on the neutral reality and the result we get.

The Thought Model I am talking about looks like this:

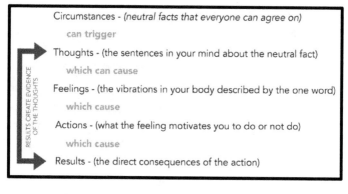

When I work with my clients in their Power Dynamics Master Certification Trainings, I shorten the thought model to look like this:

C:

T:

F:

A:

R:

In any given circumstance, there are thousands of thoughts available, and many of us have multiple thoughts about one circumstance. For example, a problem I see my clients run into quite often is debating the truth of a very negative thought or its opposite. She thinks, "I'm going to get fired from my job," and then she thinks, "I should be more positive, so I'll just tell myself, 'I'm definitely not going to get fired!'" But, "I'm definitely not going to get fired" doesn't feel believable to her, and so she believes her only option is to go back to believing that she is going to get fired.

Our brains are always inclined to go toward the negative because that is how they have evolved to protect us for thousands of years, like we talked about with the mountain lions. If you lived in a cave and are being hunted by a mountain lion, it would help you to survive to be constantly worried about the negative. But now that we are not in imminent danger of being eaten by wild animals, our brain's tendency toward the negative does not find a release in saving us from actual danger. If we can experience threat, defend ourselves from it, and escape, we feel a mental release and even exhilaration. But that is not the type of threat most of us experience anymore. Instead, when we are experiencing a conflict at work our brain is primed for a physical threat and we develop a low-level, constant anxiety that actually puts us in more danger. When we are in a constant state of anxiety, we are so distracted by perceived small problems that it actually puts us in more danger of real harm. We have dulled our instinctive fear senses so much that we are less likely to see real danger.

Even though the fact that our brains lean toward the negative means we have working brains (yay!), it is worth doing the work to retrain our unconscious brains to put ourselves in a more powerful place.

The first thing we want to do in order to do that is to validate where we are now. If you feel anxiety around the workplace culture you are creating, it is likely valid and justified. Arguing with it will not do you any good, and the worst thing that will happen is a feeling. So, for example, notice the difference between these two thought models:

Circumstance: I own a business.

Thought: I might hurt my employees.

Feeling: Worry

Action: Avoid my employees.

Result: My employees are less likely to tell me if there's a problem.

Circumstance: I own a business.

Thought: I can find information to help me with my business.

Feeling: Motivated

Action: Read this book.

Result: Learn tools that I can share to create a better company culture.

Notice how the second thought model is more positive and forward-moving, but it is not the direct opposite of the original thought. Often, we believe we have to choose a negative perspective on an issue if the opposite extreme does not feel believable. But, just because an extremely positive thought does not feel believable, it does not mean an extremely negative thought is true. In fact, neither are the objective reality. Either is simply a choice. There are thousands of other choices.

I think about it as though a circumstance is a literal rock (as opposed to Dwayne "The Rock" Johnson, although you could use him here too), that is just sitting there, and each possible thought and what it creates is like a balloon tied to the rock.

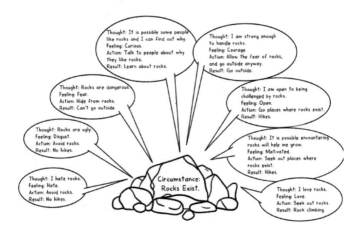

The circumstance that rocks exist remains true no matter what thought you choose about them. The same is true with every part of reality. Now, my best friend likes to say, "But what about human trafficking and child abuse? Those can't be neutral." It's true that with some circumstances we want to choose thoughts that feel negative. If my brother dies, I want to feel grief. But choices still exist. For example, many people spend so much energy believing "child abuse should not exist" that they have no energy left over to do anything to stop child abuse. Believing that abuse, harassment, discrimination, or inappropriate behavior should not exist does nothing to stop it. Acknowledging that it does exist lets us move forward to choosing a thought that will create a feeling that will motivate us to make an impact on the issues we care about.

In order to shift power dynamics, the simple truth is that we have to look at the root cause of the power imbalance: Our thoughts. Many of us were raised to be people pleasers, which is one way we learn to give our power away. People pleasing is always lying because it is not representing how we truly feel about a circumstance. Generally, we believe that if we say what another person wants to hear, that person will like us, and that will keep us safe. In reality, we don't give the other person a chance to like us because we've told them something contrary to what we actually believe. We've said "yes" when we mean "no" (or "no" when we mean "yes'). Any time we do this, it is like we are taking our Universe-given duty to protect our soul and placed it on another person. We have given our power away. Later, we are angry, as though the other person did something to us, when really we have not learned to use our power to protect ourselves.

An example of this came when I was going through my own sexual harassment experience, and I see this often with clients. When my boss would massage my shoulders or lean his body on me, I would uncomfortably laugh. I was terrified. But I had also been lectured that my boss being happy was crucial to keeping my job. And, having grown up as a people pleaser, I did not honor my duty to protect myself.

Now, I do not look back and blame myself or any other person who has not confronted a boss in that type of situation. I was genuinely preserving my safety and my job, I believed. But I had entrenched beliefs that it was not acceptable for me to say no to a man in power. I also had a recurring, nagging thought in my mind, "maybe there's something wrong with me, and I really don't deserve respect." When that thought would come up, I would argue with it and try to repress it, which turned it into an underlying unconscious assumption. I thought it was "bad" to believe I didn't deserve respect, but the thought "I do everything right and deserve respect" did not feel believable, and so I thought I was stuck with the negative belief.

It was not until I looked directly and clearly at these thoughts using the Thought Model structure that I was able to truly take action to keep myself safe. Once I questioned my people pleasing and self-defeating beliefs, I did not immediately transition into positive sunshine-and-rainbows thinking, but I was able to choose thoughts that motivated action to keep me safe. I continued reporting what my boss was doing and did not give up until I found someone with the authority he would listen to, who was willing to tell him to stop. This meant that I did not give up after the first three things I tried to get the behavior to stop. I kept going because I let go of disempowering expectations that "harassment shouldn't happen," and I embraced the belief that my career was worth protecting.

Beliefs are just thoughts we think over and over again. We have the opportunity to question whether we can absolutely know whether our thought is true, how we react when we believe our thought, and who we would be if that thought didn't exist. Once we have looked into these crucial questions and explored our other options, it becomes clearer where we are giving away our power.

Shifting Power Dynamics as a Leader

For inclusive leaders in the workplace, shifting power dynamics can be difficult in a different way. Hestia described that when she started managing people she had worked as peers with before, she stopped being invited to lunches with them. At first, she was offended and thought maybe she had done something or that someone was deliberately excluding her. Later, she realized that as the manager, people she used to consider peers now thought of her as the boss. It became her job to reach out to them to maintain relationships. Their perception of her power shifted, even though hers did not.

As a leader, helping subordinates empower themselves so that they understand they have not only permission but the duty to keep themselves safe at work, can be a key step toward creating a healthy workplace culture. Where an employer can teach an employee, without judgment, how to shift their thinking in order to go from feeling powerless to understanding where they do have power, it can dramatically change workplace culture. If an employee feels disempowered, harassed, or discriminated against and you, as a boss, do not feel comfortable teaching these tools yourself, that is totally fair and sometimes it would not be appropriate for you to teach these tools. That is where a trained coach can come in as a neutral outside party to help make the shifts that are necessary to create a healthy workplace.

This step is not about making sure that no one ever does anything harassing or discriminatory and the boss taking on all of the burden to correct that behavior. It is about empowering each employee to honor his or her own boundaries and ask for a change when there is behavior that crosses those boundaries. This usually happens best by helping employees look at any disempowering thoughts they may have that hold them back from keeping themselves safe or talking about discrimination. Sometimes, simply saying, "You know you have permission to always keep yourself safe, right?" or "I always want to hear about any room for improvement you see in our culture if you're willing to share," is enough, but often employees have cultural training and expectations that make this difficult for them to follow through with, even if they want to. Or, they can sometimes feel threatened by these questions if, for example, you are only asking people with a culturally disadvantaged characteristic. They see being confronted with a boundary violation or a discrimination issue like the mountain lion attack we were talking about earlier because most of us have had an experience of it being unsafe to talk about discrimination. It is often easy to see it as simple from outside of the situation, but for those inside of the situation it can feel like they're going up against "The Rock" in a wrestling match. When that is the case and simply giving permission is not enough, it's a signal that an employee may need a full Power Dynamics Master Certification Training, which can really help address underlying issues and make a significant shift.

Overall, the thing to remember is that when we expect people, even ourselves, to act in a discriminatory or harassing way, knowing that cognitive bias exists in all of our brains, and when we can be open to looking at that and shifting in it, we really have a chance to create healthy company culture. When we expect that some employees will have been trained by culture that it is dangerous to talk about the biases they see, we can do better to create an actually safe space for conversations around bias and harassment, without re-traumatizing employees who have experienced bias as a physical threat. It is no one's obligation to tell their story or talk about bias where they see it, but each of us can make a difference in this way if we are willing.

Takeaways:

- For someone experiencing harassment, it is *always* about power.
- Teaching harassers to stop harassing has never worked because they do not have motivation to stop.
- Teaching all employees how to understand and shift power dynamics puts them in a powerful position to stop behavior they find offensive in the moment.
- When we believe we are in a powerless place, we are more likely to have aggressive and inappropriate behavior.

- Our thoughts determine how much power we have in any circumstance. Our thoughts create our feelings.

Chapter 8: Causal Conflict Resolution

Let's be real, the news has been bleak when it comes to the opportunity for reconciliation and resolution around harassment, discrimination, and abuse. After the 2016 presidential election, many of us took a step back in disbelief, realizing how polarized the United States has become. We've seen protesters on the side of white supremacy and protesters on the side of feminism and gun control. Sometimes these protesters are in the same family circles. Throughout the country, people are shouting loudly to have their voices heard in ways that sometimes seem irreconcilable.

Many of our workplaces are microcosms of this larger picture, which can create intense and even crisis levels of conflict. If you are a boss who genuinely wants to create an inclusive, healthy environment, this puts you in a difficult position. Do you just fire everyone who disagrees politically or ideologically with you? That would be contrary to the ideals of inclusion, but unless you have a system implemented in your business to resolve crisis level conflict, sometimes it feels necessary.

Unfortunately, we look around at the current systems implemented in the United States and they are less than effective at truly resolving conflict. Sometimes, we see great politicians able to speak to both sides of the divided country and bring us together with a common goal, but seeing one person who is exceptionally good at resolving conflict doesn't help the rest of us. It is too person-specific. Barack Obama is unlikely to drop into your staff meeting to help everyone see things from another perspective.

The Root Cause of Conflict: Our Thoughts

The good news is that really anyone can learn to resolve conflict, and it starts, again, with understanding the root cause of conflict: Our thoughts. What we are thinking that motivates conflict and what we actually say to engage in conflict are often different. The way we communicate our thoughts is inaccurate even with people who generally understand us and believe the best about us.

An example of this problem looks like this:

On both sides of the conflict, we expect that the thought motivating what we are saying is completely obvious to everyone around us. We believe that all we need is for everyone else to see that we're completely reasonable and agree with us, and that will resolve the conflict.

The trouble with that expectation is that there can be multiple, reasonable interpretations of any given circumstance. If you look at the conflict example above, no one would say that either person's worry about their own position in the business was unreasonable. Fear over failing clients or losing a job can feel very real and important in the moment. But both thoughts are contributing to conflict, rather than contributing to fixing the letter problem.

This is always true in conflict. When we are focused on being *right* instead of getting our best outcome, we contribute to more conflict. This is because there can be multiple reasonable perspectives about any neutral circumstance. Both people become committed to their *one right* perspective, missing that their perspective is only one reasonable option among many. This turns into a spiral of increased, dramatic clashes, like this:

The illustrations represent an example of how in conflict we are having two completely different internal conversations that so strongly filter our experience of the external conversation as to almost make it irrelevant. If you look at this example, there is actually no problem other than a letter that could be fixed. Both parties are diving into an internal conflict spiral, though, based on their own thought about what the conversation means. Both people have reasonable motivation – the boss wants to serve her clients and the employee wants to keep her job. But they are seeing the external circumstances very differently.

Being Right versus Best Outcome

If the employee is so committed to proving that she was not at fault with the letter (that she was *right*), she will continue to engage in the conflict. Likewise, if the boss is so committed to proving that the employee needs to take responsibility (that *she* is right), she will also engage in the conflict. Instead, if both people focus on the *best outcome* and allow the other person to have a different perspective (even one that seems wrong), they will bypass the conflict.

In traditional Western conflict resolution processes, this is similar to considering the Best Alternative to a Negotiated Agreement (BATNA), described in the book *Getting to Yes*. A BATNA is somewhat self-explanatory, but it basically asks each person to consider whether it would be better to compromise their position or to go forward with the conflict. For example, if an employee wants a promotion, a boss has to consider her BATNA. Two alternatives to agreeing to the promotion are (1) say no and risk the employee leaving or (2) make a counter offer. At each stage of the negotiation, both parties need to consider whether their best alternative is better than the offer on the table. We often use BATNAs in traditional legal settlements, where a mediator walks between two rooms, encouraging one room to lower their offer and one room to raise their offer. Each side has to consider the costs and stress of walking away and going to trial versus making a new offer or accepting the offer on the table.

Parents I know often use BATNAs as an effective parenting tool. For example, they offer to their child that she can get into her car seat and be allowed to have her applesauce pouch or she can choose not to have an applesauce pouch and stay outside of the car. Parents will offer a child two options for lunch (say, a peanut butter and jelly sandwich or a cheese sandwich), rather than asking the child the open-ended question, "What do you want for lunch?" because giving alternatives allows the child to consider the best alternative.

Considering a BATNA is a basic negotiation and conflict resolution principle, but the traditional Western conflict resolution processes have failed at resolving highly-charged emotional disputes because they do not consider the thinking and feeling components to the conflict. We even see this with children when the option the parent offered becomes unavailable. If a parent offers a PB&J and then can't follow through, the process of negotiation through alternatives has essentially failed and a tantrum may be reasonably expected, even if a parent wants to go back to offering other alternatives.

Talking about negotiation with children is a simple way of looking at this, but in truth community reconciliation processes used outside of Western culture have addressed some of the deepest cultural wounds we have seen in history. Reconciliation processes such as the Hawaiian Ho'oponopono reconciliation process or the community storytelling process used by the South African Truth and Reconciliation Commission to heal the cultural wounds of apartheid have been shown to be incredibly effective, but often feel inaccessible and overly ceremonial in Western businesses. The Western negotiation model tends to focus on the individualized success of a negotiation process, while the community reconciliation model focuses on the community's bonds. Both are important in deciding what the best outcome to a conflict is, and for each person a best outcome may look different and put more weight on one or another. Sometimes an individual's best outcome includes community bonds and reconciliation.

When true cultural or personal divides exist in a conflict, one person may prefer a reconciliation model and another a negotiation model of responding. This can overly complicate the conflict and create even more division. If one person is focused on the bonds of the community, and the other is focused on external success of a negotiation, the two people often talk past each other.

For example, Grace asked me to talk with one of her employees about high-conflict behavior the employee was having and whether she could keep working for the company. In talking with the employee, it became clear that the employee wanted to do whatever it would take to keep her job (not because she needed the job, she explained, but because she did not want to be fired). But she was not willing to acknowledge her high-conflict behavior, such as yelling and talking about other employees negatively behind their backs. Grace wanted her employee to be able to engage in a restorative process to acknowledge her problem behavior and rejoin the bonds of the group. The employee, however, wanted to keep her job in order to avoid what she perceived as the humiliation of being fired. The employee was negotiating, while Grace was attempting to reconcile. They were at an impasse, and Grace ended up deciding the employee needed to be separated from the company.

Sometimes, separation is the best, most loving option in a dispute (or even without a dispute). Separation is the best option when it is a positive growth step. Other times, we feel it is our only option because of communication breakdown. Where the latter is the case, differences of communication do not need to undermine the process.

Asking Why

The one key, simple step toward resolving a conflict is asking, "why?" I know it sounds too simple to actually be useful, but it works because it is so simple. Asking why helps you stand in the other person's shoes and truly understand the Thought Models they are having that are motivating their side of the conflict. It only works if you have done your work first to understand and feel comfortable about your own perspective. Ask yourself "why" first, and make sure you like your reason for continuing the conversation. You know you have your work first if you are open and willing to say your opinion, you understand what the best outcome looks like for you, and you are more committed to the best outcome than to being right.

One of the strangest things about the results of asking "why" to another person is that you always discover that there is something reasonable, something you can have compassion for, about the other person's perspective. If you have tried asking "why" and have not found something you can have compassion for from the other side's perspective, you just have not asked "why?" enough times. Even if you still know the other person's perspective is wrong, asking "why?" creates space for you to have compassion and understanding and help the other person walk toward your perspective.

It is like two people are standing on top of their own mountains, in their own mountain fortresses of being *right*, shouting at each other. When one person asks "why?" it is her coming out of her mountain fortress and taking a step down the mountain to understand where the other person is coming from. From there, she can walk with the other person toward a shared understanding. It takes strength and security in your own perspective to be willing to ask "why?" without people pleasing or pretending to agree with something you don't. In the process of asking why, truly all you need to do is genuinely understand something reasonable about the other person's perspective. You can absolutely continue to believe the other person is wrong, but until you understand the thoughts behind what the other person is saying, you can't truly know what you are disagreeing with.

Put your argument on pause and just listen, even though it is hard and you believe the other person is the one who needs to listen to you. If there is space and the person you are talking with is willing to answer, get permission from them to ask questions and ask "why?" five times or ten times. This is the hardest part of truly being curious – stepping out of your own argument. Do not try to explain *your* perspective until the other person asks or you offer and get consent to do so. Explaining your position is not helpful, understanding the other person's perspective is. You lose the Why Game if you try to explain your position before you can accurately reflect the other person's position. However many times it takes for you to find something that seems genuinely reasonable to you, ask "why" until you find that thing. Usually, we all agree on core points of safety, security, feeding our families, and caring about the people who are important to us. We disagree about how to do that, and our disagreements are genuine, so I am not encouraging you to pretend you agree where you don't. I am only offering this tool as a starting point.

The other person does not need to believe in Ho'oponopono in order to appreciate someone caring about why she's taken the position she has. Having someone genuinely want to understand our perspective is a starting point for resolving conflict no matter the communication patterns or beliefs of either person.

At the beginning of the book, I talked about Rhea's situation where one employee accused another of sexual harassment. When I sat with them and asked them why they were taking the position they did, both responded from some sense of shame about themselves. The man who felt he was sexually harassed believed he was in a disadvantaged position in the company and that he was powerless in his life in general. The woman who was accused also had victimizing experiences and saw herself as disadvantaged in the situation and as vulnerable to the man's accusations. Both saw each other as a threat to their jobs. When they could shift and see themselves in a more powerful place, they were also better able to see the other person's perspective with compassion and feel confident about keeping themselves safe.

When we ask why and try genuinely to understand, we can see our mountain from the other person's perspective. We can stand in their shoes, even if we decide those shoes are not a good fit for us in the long run. When we can discover the thoughts behind her actions, we are in a better place to help her understand why those thoughts are not serving her, if that is indeed the case.

Often, asking "why?" sounds disingenuous to us because we expect other people to have the same thoughts as us. What I have found since I have started working on these resolution processes is that we all have incredibly different thoughts and reasoning behind what we do. I often preface my questions to clients by saying, "I am not pretending to be dumb, or trying to make a point, but I genuinely want to make sure I understand why. I've discovered in my work with people that if I make an assumption about a particular person's reasoning, I will often get it wrong." The purpose of asking "why" is to genuinely understand and stop making assumptions. It is not to play dumb so that we can trap someone else in thinking errors. Until you can genuinely, openly ask "why?" you know you have your own work to do in questioning your own thoughts and shifting power dynamics to understand that you have power in the situation.

Again, you need to be confident in your own power in the situation, and have worked on your own thoughts and like the reason for your perspective first, before you ask a person you're in conflict with why they are acting the way they are. This is a tool for someone who is in a power position in a conflict situation, not for someone who feels disadvantaged. When we feel powerless, we often see other people's perspectives and accept them above our own. Criticizing and diminishing our own perspective is generally more destructive and likely to lead to conflict than failing to understand another person's perspective.

Cycles of Conflict

Conflict is always optional. And by that I mean that not only is it never necessary to choose conflict, it is also your choice if you *do* want to choose conflict. Many people unconsciously or consciously enjoy the charge of conflict and find it stimulating. After all, many of us choose to be competitive athletes, politicians, or trial lawyers and actively engage in adversarial disputes. We enjoy the process of conflict. You are not required to resolve conflict, ever. It is always your choice.

At its best, perpetual conflict can become the pressure that creates a diamond or the chiseling that makes a smooth stone. A flower has to break open the shell of its seed to grow. There are many positive metaphors in nature for stress and conflict being a positive force of growth.

At its worst, perpetual conflict can become a cycle of abuse or an addiction. The cycle of violence theory, developed by Dr. Lenore Walker, describes the process that most abusive relationships become trapped in that perpetuate violence. That process looks like this:

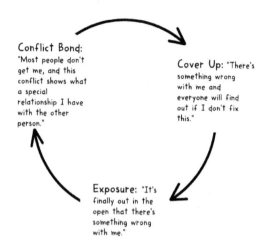

Conflict Bond: "Most people don't get me, and this conflict shows what a special relationship I have with the other person."

Cover Up: "There's something wrong with me and everyone will find out if I don't fix this."

Exposure: "It's finally out in the open that there's something wrong with me."

This process is an extreme version of what many of us experience when we're caught in a conflict situation. It sounds "bad" or unhealthy to call it a cycle of abuse, and many of us resist identifying when we could be caught in an unhealthy cycle because it seems so disempowering. In reality, though, much if not all of the unhealthiness comes from our own internal process, which we do have control over (even when it doesn't seem that way). For example, from the outside, I have often seen people, even healthcare professionals, encounter a woman caught in a cycle of abuse and say to her, "Well, you can just leave, so there's not a problem." This fails to understand the internal cycle of abuse we go through when we are caught in conflict. Once we resolve the internal cycle of abuse, the external cycle of abuse as shown above naturally resolves. The internal cycle of abuse usually looks something like this:

This is an oversimplification of the thinking process for both parties, but when two people are engaged in perpetual conflict, this internal cycle is often pretty similar on both the instigator side and the receiver side. Often in a relationship (personal or professional) that has perpetual conflict, both sides believe the other is instigating the conflict, whether that belief is reasonable or not. Both sides wait for the other to change and demand the other to change, even when that fails to work over and over again.

One woman I worked with who was in an abusive romantic relationship returned to that relationship over and over again (this is very common, and some research says that an average relationship takes about eight to sixteen times to leave permanently). This woman understood it was dangerous to return to the relationship, and her boyfriend had been convicted of multiple crimes. Nevertheless, she was caught in this internal cycle of self-abuse and, because her boyfriend's abuse was consistent with her beliefs about herself, it was falsely comfortable to return to that relationship.

I see this often with employees who truly do become career refugees or who stay in abusive jobs without taking steps to create safety for themselves. One woman I worked with explained to me that she had always been a victim, and so she could never support herself and her daughters, always needing to rely on a boyfriend's support. She had gone from relationship to relationship, experiencing everything from physical violence to infidelity to ridicule. When she trained for a job she was passionate about, her instructor sexually assaulted and harassed her for months before she left the program. But, even when she was away from this abuse, her beliefs about herself were equally abusive. The abuse she experienced on the outside was obviously not caused by her thoughts and her self-abuse, but it was not inconsistent with her beliefs about herself, and so she tolerated it longer than someone would have whose internal world was self-nurturing or confident. Her self-abuse pattern allowed her to feel like dangerous situations were more comfortable than safe, respectful ones. Through intense work, she shifted to seeing how her self-abusive patterns were not serving her and keeping her in danger.

On the other hand, I have seen employees stay for twenty years in jobs that were actively dangerous and where they were underpaid. One woman explained to me that she historically made approximately $10,000 less per year than a less experienced male co-worker and she saw men actively threaten women in her workplace to the point where one woman was murdered by a male co-worker outside of the workplace. But it was still scarier to this woman to think about challenging the system and stepping out of the patterns that kept her stuck in abuse.

Often, the reason we engage in these patterns is that they have kept us safe somehow in dangerous situations, and our brains start to see them as safety. For example, even though they had both been physically threatened, the women I described above have not died yet by sticking with their self-abusive patterns. Their brains have not seen what it looks like to shift patterns, and so they see any shift as a threat.

Even in less extreme scenarios, it can feel impossible to make a shift without outside support. The reason for this goes back to the problem of power dynamics. When both sides see themselves (reasonably or unreasonably) as victims, they justify increasingly bad behavior. After all, if you are a sugar ant, your strongest attack against an elephant will do no good, so you have to go above and beyond your strongest attack to defend yourself if you see yourself in that powerless place. We live in a culture that teaches men to externalize conflict and teaches women to internalize responsibility for conflict. For example, in the United States we see more terrorist mass shootings from young white men than any other group. This is not because of their natural physical makeup, but because they have been taught to externalize their inner process or blame what they view as going wrong in the world on other people. These shooters believe they are justified in their terrorist attacks because of what they have been taught to expect from life. Men also have higher rates of suicide than women in the United States, which is another externalized expression of a conflict cycle. Women, by contrast, have higher rates than men in the United States of problems related to internalizing, like depression, anxiety, and eating disorders. Each of these problems, in men and women, are only a symptom of the underlying thinking.

There is nothing inherently wrong with conflict where it is not actually dangerous, and often conflict can lead to growth. I named my business after the Greek goddess of discord, Eris, and a quote from her in the *Principia Discordia* says, "I am the substance from which your artists and scientists build rhythms. I am the spirit with which your children and clowns laugh in happy anarchy. I am chaos. I am alive, and I tell you that you are free." Many of us who were raised in a household where we were not allowed to disagree with adults find conflict refreshing and freeing. That is different than destructive conflict, whether the destruction is to yourself or to others.

Destructive conflict can become addictive because our brains create certain neural connections and like to retread them over and over again for efficiency. When we are repeating patterns of cover up, exposure, and conflict bonds, our brains get addicted to them, releasing hormones associated with reward, even while we are participating in something scary or self-destructive. We start to work against ourselves and become increasingly self-destructive because we have associated that pattern with satisfying a need.

As with any addiction, an addiction to over-conflict or over-drama can be intentionally shifted and redirected to something positive. It does not mean that you have to roll over and just agree with what anyone else says, be a doormat, or pretend your opinions are different than they are. It also does not mean that it should be easy, obvious, or that you should be able to do this on your own. Conflict is a normal part of life, and when we are particularly resistant to allowing any conflict in life, we can stagnate. When we are addicted to over-conflict, it can become destructive.

One important first step is to question any assumptions you might have that there is something wrong with you or with reality just as it is. When we are struggling with who we are or with what reality is, we are disempowering ourselves and creating an internal conflict. The external conflict we have is only a manifestation of what is going on inside. If you are experiencing conflict in your workplace, what is a belief you have about yourself that you may be able to question that could shift the way you are encountering the conflict? Where is there room for you to understand the other person's unspoken thoughts about the conflict?

Another important step is to understand what are appropriate conflicts for you to resolve yourself and where it is important to bring in outside support. It is not always appropriate for a business owner or manager to resolve a conflict, especially if you have an opinion about the right outcome. Realistically, it is also not always an effective use of your time. If you feel stuck in a conflict situation it may be worth bringing in outside support to help both sides understand and shift the power dynamics of the conflict.

Takeaways:

- The root cause of conflict is our thinking.
- What someone says in conflict and what we make it mean are often two very different things.
- Wanting to be *right* creates more conflict; working toward a *best outcome* bypasses conflict.
- In order to resolve conflict, we have to resolve our conflicted, self-defeating thinking. We start by asking ourselves and the person we're in conflict with

"why?" until we can genuinely understand and have compassion for both perspectives.

- Conflict can be good, productive, and inspire creativity and growth. Addiction to perpetual conflict can be destructive. Resolving that starts with resolving our internal conflict, which shows up as resistance to who we are or to what reality is.

Chapter 9: Transparency

Before you owned your business, did you ever work in a business where it seemed like the rules were written by Lucy in *Charlie Brown*? Every time you're just sure you're going to kick the football out of the park, someone moves it and you fall flat on your behind. That is the challenge of working for a business where transparency is not a priority. Only Lucy feels comfortable and safe. Employees start withdrawing and hesitating to share their creative ideas and opinions. They start playing it safe and only completing the minimum requirements of their jobs. I talked with a manager in a business once, for example, who told me that she had no designated budget for her projects, and so she had no idea whether she was spending too much or too little. Rather than making her feel free to create what she wanted, she felt oppressed and insecure about the expectations. She knew she could do something wrong and not find out until after the fact because the parameters of her work were not clear. Because shifting expectations, rewards, and punishments foster insecurity in employees, it also nurtures an environment in which harassment and discrimination have opportunities to infect the culture.

Most businesses say they believe in transparency, but following through with being transparent can often feel painful and confusing, and therefore many businesses do not actually follow through with being transparent either with their clients or with their employees. Like with acknowledging cultural health issues, transparency can often feel like a threat to privacy, individual achievements, tradition, or hierarchy. The reality is that, even though it doesn't have to be a threat to those priorities, it often can be depending on how we execute a plan for transparency. A poorly executed plan for transparency can make people feel targeted or isolated within a company culture, and so it is important to plan ahead of time for how transparency could impact employees and bosses in your business. For example, releasing budget information for different projects within a company can be an important step of transparency. But if one employee's project is underfunded compared to others that can create dissatisfaction or the impression that the employee is disfavored. If that actually is the case, it is better for that information to be in the open than hidden so that the employee has the chance to correct any problems contributing to that disfavoring. If the imbalanced funding is simply an oversight, correcting the imbalance ahead of time can prevent isolating or targeting an employee. Either way, talking with the employee ahead of time in a productive way can prevent the shock of a sudden release of information to the rest of the group.

Transparency is not just a financial issue, though. Transparency can also be key when it comes to promotional opportunities and challenging employees to excel within the business. Whitney Johnson, in her research at Harvard Business School, developed a framework of learning that she calls Disruption. She explains that our learning is based on an s-curve, and cites E.M. Rogers in his work on *Diffusion of Innovations*. She explains that the s-curve of Disruption looks like this:

The research shows that growth is slow at first, with a huge spike once we reach the "competence point" or the "tipping point." After that huge spike, growth slows again as the task we are performing becomes very easy and even boring. Employees are vulnerable to leaving a business at the bottom of the s-curve, when growth is very difficult, and at the top of the s-curve, when tasks become very easy. Johnson recommends "disrupting" our tasks with new challenges at the top of the s-curve in order to bring challenges when work has become too easy.

Johnson estimates that when someone has been in a role for six months to a year, they are at the low end of the s-curve. When someone has been in a role for three or four years, she estimates they are at the high end of the s-curve and in the "danger zone." At that point, it is important to allow the employee to jump to a new learning curve (a new s-curve) so that they re-engage and experience challenge.

When a business is not transparent and deliberate about advancement opportunities for employees, it risks losing employees at the top of the s-curve. This can be very expensive because it is losing employees just when they are mastering their role, becoming very efficient, and when the business' early investment in the employee is paying off.

Creating Advancement Transparency

In order to create transparency in an employee's opportunities for advancement, I have businesses that I provide a Cultural Health Facilitation for complete Career Maps for each position within the business. A career map can be as simple as this:

Receptionist > Assistant > Associate > Division Manager > General Manager > Director > Franchise Owner > Multiple Franchise Owner

It also includes the objective requirements each position needs to demonstrate in order to be promoted to the next level of the business. You are the one who knows best what you want from those roles in order for an employee to move on to the next promotion, but it is important for the requirements to be objectively measurable and binary. What I mean is that you need to have a clear yes or no about whether the employee has completed the requirement. The career map should track from the position in question all the way to the highest level of what is possible in your industry. If you are an entrepreneur, the map should light the path for how someone stepping into a receptionist role could ultimately become her own entrepreneur in a business like yours or by expanding your business.

You may be thinking that some receptionists stay in their role for decades and are amazing at what they do. Think about Mrs. Landingham in *The West Wing*, who charmingly and humbly went from administrator in a school to administrator in the White House. She seemed so happy! The problem with this idea is that it does not track with the research about how employees can be most effective and engaged. Some people definitely do stay in positions and move laterally, without challenging themselves to something more difficult. Other people find challenges outside of work and are not interested in pursuing challenging careers, but are happy in that "mastery" and "boredom" place on the s-curve.

What you want to ask yourself is whether those are the employees that you want to be designing your business around. Do you want to be catering to employees who prefer stagnation to challenge or to employees who look for growth? Often, business owners are unconsciously catering to employees who avoid challenge without ever making a decision about it. We do this by hiring employees into roles that have no advancement plan or opportunities. We do this by avoiding employees who challenge the systems and assumptions we have in place.

As a society, we have recognized how important it is to have employees in the workplace who challenge systems that are not working or that are breaking the law, and so we have implemented whistleblower and anti-retaliation laws. Those laws are limited, however, and they do not require business owners to embrace employees who challenge us to grow and question our assumptions. When we can deliberately plan ahead of time to create a business environment where employees who seek out challenge are able to find it, we use their energy in our favor instead of becoming defensive against it.

Creating Transparency in Discipline and Termination

In most states in the United States, employment is "at will," meaning that an employee can be fired for any reason, unless the reason is specifically prohibited by law. Sometimes, employees have access to a union, which provides more protection for them, but generally businesses that have reached success and started scaling have hired employees who do not have access to those protections. Much of what a union enforces, though, is simply transparency, and this can often be as much of an advantage to an employer as to an employee. For example, it can seem more efficient to be able to fire someone without jumping through the hoops of clear discipline and setting transparent expectations, and that is technically legal in the majority of situations. The problem is that following that practice inevitably creates insecurity and gossip in the rest of the company. As we talked about earlier, this insecurity can contribute to not only the sense of victimization and being targeted, it can also contribute to encouraging insecure employees to harass others.

While this type of fear about others' perceptions may be internally motivated and controlled, there are also work environments that foster this type of insecurity. When rewards and punishments appear unpredictable and leaders use favoritism in an attempt to motivate competition, it also fosters an environment of harassment and discrimination.

Having clear, transparent, externally measurable expectations, disciplinary steps, and guidelines for behavior (both behavior that deserves promotion or reward and behavior that deserves discipline) nurtures the kind of job security that can significantly reduce or stop harassment and discrimination. You may not know what these are right away, and part of transparency is being open about your own process in developing what your business structure is.

You will get this wrong. Have clear, compassionate expectations for yourself like you would for another employee you care about. You are your own boss, too. Learning how to be a real leader is supposed to be hard.

I recommend following these three rules, and expecting your employees to do the same:

1. Be kind.
2. Be respectful.
3. Do your work.

In the Employee Handbook I offer at www.ErisResolution.com/handbook, I explain and give examples of what it means to be kind and respectful in case they do seem vague. Some people were raised with different expectations about what it means to be kind and respectful, and I always encounter conflict situations expecting those definitions to be varied. But if an employee understands your definition of what the rules mean, she can decide whether a shared definition works for her. If she is not a good fit for an employment situation where she is expected to be kind, respectful, and do her work (and you as a leader/employee are expected to do the same), then it may be better for her to work somewhere else. If she believes in the values of kindness, respect, and hard work, a transparent culture can be a place where she is allowed to make mistakes, learn, and grow, without being ostracized from the community.

I also recommend that an underlying expectation of "no touching" without affirmative, active consent be the expectation of the workplace. Like I discussed in previous chapters, this makes your workplace oriented to be a safe place for employees who may have experienced physical trauma in the past, rather than catering to employees who may have bad boundaries. It does not completely prohibit anyone from touching, although in general touching co-workers seems unnecessary and often is just creepy. But there are instances where a warm hug between co-workers is totally appropriate, and this rule just designates how to do that in a way that feels safe for everyone. It lets an employee, who may feel uncomfortable with touching in the workplace, know that if she declines to be touched, she will be respected rather than ridiculed and retaliated against.

Are transparent expectations and discipline a cure-all for turnover in employees? They are not, and I actually think that is a good thing. Sometimes, it is appropriate to terminate someone's employment or for that person to quit. This is generally a painful experience, and that is okay – it is not meant to be exciting or happy. You may have concerns around hurting someone's income, and the amount of power you have around that. Those concerns are fair and helpful to own. But it does not have to be a traumatic or horrible experience. Ultimately, when you are active about creating an inclusive, safe workplace, a good enough reason to separate an employee is that one of you wants that. If you like your job-related reason for retaining an employee, do it. If you like your job-related reason for separating with an employee, also do it.

Often, when we think an employment relationship is not working, we only let ourselves end the relationship after things have gotten so terrible that they are intolerable. You see this in romantic relationships too. "It's not bad enough to get a divorce, we just don't talk or have sex anymore." Then, you see each person unconsciously working toward making the relationship more and more intolerable. We go to friends and try to prove that the relationship is bad enough to leave, and we develop a narrative about the relationship being terrible. That narrative contributes to a worse and worse experience, in a relationship that was already bad.

Let yourself end any relationship that is not working, romantic, platonic, or business, just because you want to end it. You don't need any excuse. If something is not working toward what you want in your life, it is okay to let it go.

The hard part about letting yourself end a relationship because you want to is that you have to take responsibility that it is what you want. Ending any relationship does have an impact. But ending a relationship because you want to is a responsible way to take care of yourself and take care of your work.

Know why you want to end the relationship, and if you like your reason, that is good enough. Don't let yourself be satisfied with reasons like, "There's just something wrong," or "this is just a bad fit." Those reasons are surface level and tend to be a cloak for our brain's unconscious bias. A vague sense that there is something wrong, without digging deeper, often is a signal that we have a different cultural background than the other person. Sometimes, though, it is our unconscious brain signaling that there is a danger. Many times, after significant fraud or safety issues at work, people look back and say they knew there was "something wrong" with the perpetrator of a crime. Even more often, though, women and minorities are fired because they are the "wrong fit" with a culturally homogenous group of white men. It is not only white men whose brains have unconscious bias; they just tend to have more power and privilege in our current culture.

All of our brains have unconscious bias and as a leader in your business, your unconscious bias has impact.

Bring what is unconscious forward and examine it. Know your reason for ending the relationship before you do. Bring it forward with compassion for yourself, too. Many compassionate business owners allow employment relationships to go on for way too long in ways that impact their work because they are not willing to have a hard conversation. This does not help the employee or your clients. We often don't want to hurt anybody else and we view ending an employment relationship (like breaking up with a romantic partner) as hurting them. The problem with this is that allowing either relationship to continue under false pretenses is also hurtful. Do you want someone to continue in a relationship with you out of pity? Most of us do not want that. Some of us do, and when that is the case, it is usually because we do not understand our own worth. Maintaining a relationship out of pity undermines someone else's self-worth; it does not help them understand their worth.

Know where you offer charity and pro bono work. Offering gifts out of love is wonderful and has its own reward. A charity or pro bono relationship is different than an employment relationship. If your employee (or your romantic partner for that matter, but that's a different book) believes you are in a voluntary, reciprocal relationship, and you believe you are offering charity or pro bono work, there is a power imbalance infection that is unhealthy. This is an area where transparency can heal that infection instead of just covering it up and allowing it to fester until it's unbearable.

How do you know if something needs discipline or if it's unreasonable? First, you get very specific about your reason for wanting to discipline or fire someone versus not discipline and retain that person. Then you consider whether you like your reason.

One important consideration to make is whether your reason for discipline is personal and ego-related or whether it is job-related and consistent with serving your clients. Ego is not bad. Our ego tells us our preferences and our sensitivities. When we let ego take over, we become completely incapacitated and shut off from the world. We become unable to encounter anything that is different from our preferences. Pema Chodron describes ego as a perfect room in which everything is to our exact taste. The temperature is exactly right, the food is our favorite, our favorite music is playing, and the furniture is perfectly comfortable. Then, we hear something outside, so we shut the window. Smells still come from under the door, so we put towels down at all the doors. Our neighbors are loud, so we brick up the wall. Pretty soon we're trapped in our perfect room. Ego becomes a trap, but it is also a signal of where we are and what our preferences are. Encountering employees who hook us and raise issues for us is a beautiful place to question our ego.

Disciplining someone can be a wonderful way to teach them how to better serve the company and help them understand consequences. If you can understand exactly why the employee's behavior is not meeting expectations around serving clients, you can explain that to the employee and help them see the consequences.

Reinforcing, or rewarding, behavior and instruction have been shown to be consistently more effective in changing behavior, however, than discipline. When employees are afraid of a punishment, they are focused on avoiding the punishment, not focused on performing their work effectively. This makes their brain actually focus on the thing you don't want them to do, rather than the thing you do want them to do. When I tell you, "Don't think about a purple elephant," what do you think about? A purple elephant. When an employee is focused on a reward, that is more likely to be consistent with getting their work done and serving clients. One way to understand effective rewards for employees is to do what behaviorists call a *functional behavior analysis* on the employee's behavior. This means that you consider *why* the employee is acting the way she is, and provide rewards consistent with what she is looking for.

Typical rewards are tangible (food or money), attention (more interaction and praise for the employee), and escape (time off, reassignment of an undesirable project). People like some rewards better than others based on their individual ego preference. This is not a bad thing, but it is something to understand about the particular individual employee egos you are interacting with and also about yourself. Are you more comfortable giving certain types of rewards than others? Is it easy for you to arrange for time off for employees, but hard for you to see overtime on an employee's timesheet? Is it easy for you to give a Christmas bonus, but hard when an employee doesn't want to follow through with a tedious project? These are ego points for you to be aware of in yourself. They indicate where you have work to do on your own assumptions about your business and your business culture – not because any of them are wrong or right or because some rewards are better than others, but only because you will have employees who are motivated by rewards that you are uncomfortable giving. They may be valuable employees who contribute significantly to the important work you do. Where problems with an employee show you that your ego discomfort is getting in the way of your business being effective, it is worth questioning your assumptions and developing some space around your ego's sensitivity.

Ultimately, if you do want to fire an employee and you like your reason for it, transparency is important in the firing process. This doesn't mean that you need to have a public shaming of the employee, but only that you are honest with the employee about your reasons for the termination and that you take responsibility that you like those reasons and they are important to you. They can be any reasons (unless they are illegal reasons – but even then, if you choose to fire an employee for an illegal reason, at least be honest about it and pay the fines and remedies necessary to take responsibility for your decision to break the law). If you can stand in your own integrity about your decision to discipline an employee, reward an employee, or end an employment relationship, it honors your business and is respectful to the employee.

Creating Financial Transparency

Money and sex are two areas that many of us have enormous shame around. Unfortunately, secrecy around money and sex has perpetuated huge cultural betrayals against disadvantaged groups. I spoke with a forensic psychiatrist once about a case in which I represented a young woman who was sexually assaulted by a massage therapist. The psychiatrist explained to me that the research shows that people have the highest instances of post-traumatic stress disorder (PTSD) in situations of war and sexual violation and it is likely because of the moral stigma we culturally place on those issues. Where people experience traumas in areas that are not morally stigmatizing, there are fewer instances of PTSD, he explained. For example, this would indicate that when a drunk driver causes a car wreck, the person injured by the drunk driver is more likely to have PTSD than a person injured in the same way by a driver who was not drunk.

The moral stigma perpetuated by puritanical ideas that women should be sexually "pure" or that religious leaders cannot commit sexual crimes promotes secrecy and contributes to fostering a culture of sexual crimes. Just talking about sexual violations does a lot to change this culture. These are hard conversations, but we have to be able to talk about sex, even when it is hard, in order to raise a safer generation coming after us. It is okay if it takes personal work to get to a place where it is possible to talk about these issues, but it is worth doing that work to contribute to a safer culture.

Secrecy around money is similar and contributes to enormous inequality. The Institute for Women's Policy Research reports that in 2017, women overall made approximately $0.81 cents to the dollar that white men made in full-time work. Hispanic women made $0.62 and black women made $0.67 compared to a dollar for white men. It estimates that at the rate the pay gap is currently closing, we will not reach fair wages in the United States until 2059.

A major factor in why the wage gap has remained for so long is lack of transparency in wages. It was only recently that states started passing laws to correct this, making it illegal to retaliate against an employee for talking about their own or other employees' salaries, and making it more possible for employees to negotiate from an informed place. This is an important shift that can make a real impact on employees understanding what fair wages are and pursuing them. Websites like PayScale and GlassDoor contribute to this, giving employees information about whether their salary is fair in their industry. Since I have started providing Cultural Health Surveys to companies, one interesting thing I have encountered is that employees, based on lack of information within their company, will frequently believe they are being paid fairly within their industry, but unfairly within their company. Often, this is only based on lack of transparency within the company and incorrect gossip about what other employees receive as a salary. This is easy to correct, and if all employee salaries are available, it should not implicate any privacy problems. Check with a lawyer in your state if you are concerned about this, but in general employees don't have privacy protections and concerns around discrimination take priority over privacy concerns.

In government organizations, we require transparency in public salaries to prevent corruption and fraud, and we should expect no less from ourselves as private business owners. If you are concerned about transparency around salary, be curious about why. If the reason is that the salaries do not seem fair or seem to show favoritism if you look at them all together, that is something you can correct. If it is because of shame around money, that is something worth working on for yourself.

If you move toward financial transparency in terms of employee salary, the first step is making sure that the finances seem fair and represent equality and the inclusion you want to create in your company. Make sure you understand the rational reason for the salaries you are offering and feel good about those reasons (even if you wish you could pay more or less) so that you can explain them to others.

Salary is only one step toward transparency, and there is a lot of power in creating financial transparency throughout your business and allowing your employees to have stake and ownership in the successes and failures of finances throughout the company. Money is one marker of what is succeeding and failing in a business, and it is not the only marker. Money is a measurable marker, however, and that makes it a good symbol for other measures within your company that might feel more powerful or important to you.

When businesses are secretive about their profits and losses, often it is with the intent of hiding failures and promoting successes. This can be for legitimate business reasons of keeping a business open and creating the narrative you want about your company. But too often, secrecy about a business's finances actually creates suspicion and negative gossip. When employees do not understand how their employer receives funding and uses that funding, it leaves room for them to assume the worst and worry about being fired. That financial insecurity promotes fear about whether others will view them as competent, which then contributes to employees justifying harassing and discriminatory behavior.

The logistics of financial transparency are as simple as sitting down with your team, going over the real numbers in your company, and creating measured pay steps for each position in your company that are openly disclosed and freely discussed. The reality of creating financial transparency is that you may need to develop the skill of holding space for your feelings and for other people's. Finances can feel loaded because of our thoughts about money and about what our lives and our businesses should look like, but, again, you are not your thoughts, and it is possible to examine and shift them. Any feelings that you or your employees have about a shift to transparency are likely valid, but that doesn't mean the feelings have to rule the day or force you to hide.

Ultimately, money is just a circumstance. It is neutral and sits there while we choose consciously or unconsciously what to think about it. If you have trade secret or business competition concerns, it is possible to have employees agree to confidentiality regarding some parts of financial transparency. But, in the end, our decisions about whether to disclose or hide our finances always have more to do with our fears around what transparency would mean about us than any real threat to our business.

Takeaways:

- Transparency in the form of career maps for employees allows them to transition to more challenging jobs when they reach the stagnation point after three or four years in their current role.
- Transparency in the form of evenly applied, consistent rewards for job-related performance and clear rules with evenly applied discipline (if

necessary) contribute to greater productivity in employees.

- If you decide to terminate an employment relationship, understand your reason for doing it, and make sure you like your reason enough that you feel comfortable taking responsibility for it with the employee.
- Wage transparency contributes to greater equality and fairness in wages.
- Financial transparency in a business contributes to greater employee security and buy-in regarding the business's success.
- It is hard to talk about transparency, especially around issues like discrimination, sex, and money, but it is worth doing the hard work to bring these issues into the light.

Chapter 10: Long-Term Cultural Health

When I first started working with clients to resolve crisis conflict situations and sexual harassment, I saw my clients feel better so immediately that I became very optimistic that they could make permanent changes in only a couple of weeks. A month later, my clients would come back to me with the same problems and pain they had started with. The reality is that the process of rewiring our brains and questioning our biases is not an overnight process. I wish I could tell you that there was a magic elixir you could take that would suddenly help everyone see power dynamics and biases clearly. If you find it, definitely let me know.

What I teach is the closest I have ever seen to that, but it takes work and is not supposed to be immediate and easy. When we can capture the power of taking responsibility for our own feelings and the impact we make on the world, it can feel like a huge transformation, but the thought patterns we have practiced take daily work to change.

More than that, we often cannot and are not supposed to be able to see our own biases and thinking errors clearly. When a leader tries to intervene with employees, it can be productive and helpful, up to the point that the leader's own expectations and biases cloud her ability to be objective.

When there is a conflict at work, so much of resolving it is about staying in a non-judgmental watcher place and allowing both sides to have painful thoughts and feelings, while listening with compassion. That is a challenging goal, to say the least, for a business owner who just wants her employees to get over it and focus on work. It is also fair to want your employees to get over the drama and focus on work, and pretending to be flexible or compassionate, when you actually feel frustrated and annoyed, does not work. People see it right away, and it shuts down any resolution process that could contribute to real cultural health changes in your workplace.

You need to honor, express, and question your own perspective and your own role in any conflict, as a leader. Some of us expect ourselves to set aside our feelings and focus on work, but that is setting aside part of our humanity and part of what makes us great at work. When we practice setting aside our feelings and our perspective too often, there gets to be a build-up and congestion of backlogged feelings that produce constant, daily anxiety. You feeling anxious because you have a backlog of feelings contributes to more conflict, not less. Becoming emotionally constipated by setting aside your experience and feelings over and over again does not help other people feel better or create a safe space for them. It is important to honor and process your feelings in order to be able to move forward and interact in a positive way with a conflict situation.

Feelings are the key component to resolving conflict and shifting power dynamics. You have to know when you can genuinely hold space for your employees to have painful feelings, and when you are not the right person to do that. You know how, when you have a problem, it can feel very cathartic to talk to a friend about it, but she won't always give you the best advice because she is invested in the outcome – but you can sometimes talk to an outside person like an advisor or a counselor, and their opinion feels less biased? It is the same situation with you and your employees. You are invested in the outcome of a conflict, and so it is completely normal and fair if you are not the right person to resolve the conflict. Just the fact that you *want the conflict to resolve* can make it more difficult for you to hold space for everyone to have a difficult conversation.

I see this challenge come up at each step of this process. For business owners, it can be very difficult to find out about problems at the diagnostic step after a Cultural Health Survey. I have seen business owners cry when hearing about a problem, even when the problems an employee reports turn out to have been already solved. We want our employees to be happy, healthy, and productive, and it is hard to hear and process our feelings around problems our employees report that don't seem fair.

It can be very difficult to maintain confidentiality in a situation where one employee feels like she is in danger, but you know the accused person and you aren't afraid of him at all. Because you are inside of the experience, you have a valuable, on-the-ground perspective that deserves respect, but that makes it much more difficult to understand a perspective that is different than your own.

A friend lived with me a few years back, when she was trying to get away from an abusive boyfriend. When she would talk about the boyfriend, it was like hearing her describe someone I had never met – an imposing, terrifying, manipulative terrorist. When I saw her boyfriend, he just seemed like a doofus to me. I had zero fear of him.

This is why it's so important to understand that our perspective of power dynamics is going to be different than someone else's. When an employee reports a problem with someone else at work, you can assume that she feels somewhat powerless in the situation – that is why she is coming to you. She views you as having the highest amount of power, and she likely views herself as powerless, like my friend with the abusive boyfriend. Even if you see the person she's having trouble with as a doofus, she does not see that person that way.

It may be that you have all the skills necessary to step out of your own perspective and help her understand her own power, feel confident to create safety for herself, and ask for behavior she wants at work. But if that is not the case and you feel like you can't understand her perspective or like there is something unreasonable about it, you may not be the right person to resolve the conflict. There is nothing shameful or wrong about that, you just want to be careful to know whether you are the right person to get involved or whether you need to bring in outside support.

Sometimes, you may feel like your values conflict with understanding your employee's perspective. For example, we have seen in the news conflicts around whether bakers should be required to bake wedding cakes for gay couples if they do not believe in gay marriage and whether employers should be required to offer health insurance that provides birth control if the employer does not believe in birth control. On the other hand, should an employer be required to allow an employee to have time off to attend a religious rally that promotes gun violence or listen to an employee's explanation of why women and minorities should be given less respect than white men?

These are somewhat extreme situations, but are just a handful of examples of situations where a leader may have her own personal views that make it incredibly challenging for her to non-judgmentally consider all perspectives. What if you do not believe in abortion, but the employee who wants to have an abortion is also your best copywriter and hardest worker? What if you believe strongly in gun control, but the employee who is promoting gun violence is the best sales person in your office?

These examples do not even scratch the surface of the layers that conflict can take in the workplace. These issues deserve deliberate consideration and good answers, not silence and confusion. If you face a situation like this in which you have strong opinions and feelings, it is time to do your own work on that situation to be very clear about the result you want to get. Make sure you like the reason you want that result. It is *always* helpful to have an outside, unbiased, non-judgmental person to help you do that work, like it is helpful for your employees to have that resource.

It would be so great if conflict would just disappear or resolve on its own if we just ignored it and waited. It would also be so wonderful if I could get a PhD in art by taking a nap with my head on a book of art history or if I became a marathon runner by watching Netflix. Unfortunately, that is not how the universe works, and getting a PhD, becoming a marathon runner, and resolving conflict to create a healthy workplace culture all take acknowledgment of the problem and work toward a solution. The reality is that ignoring conflict and workplace cultural health issues makes them fester, grow, and interfere with employees' ability to do their jobs or even keep their jobs.

I spoke with an in-house-counsel attorney just an hour ago, and he said, "When I see employees in this situation, I think there's nothing we can do to make them happy, so they will need to leave." That is a bleak outlook on the communities we create at work, and I do not agree with it. I believe that the reason an employee should leave a job is that she wants to leave for something way better. I do not believe it is ever necessary for an employee to leave out of unhappiness or stress. I think there is always a solution in those situations.

If the experience feels emotionally charged to you, you are not the right person to resolve it. It may be better to designate someone in your organization as a trained Power Dynamics Facilitator, who is trained and willing to sit with all perspectives in a conflict to bring resolution or it may be better to work with someone externally who can approach things from a genuinely nonjudgmental place.

When I work with businesses, I make sure to sit with each person in a conflict separately for enough time to thoroughly hear their story. I do not interject with my own opinion or my own knowledge or start questioning their perspective until I have been able to repeat their perspective to them in a way that they feel is accurate. Often, being thoroughly heard and understood is the biggest component of what an employee is looking for in talking about an experience she has had.

Then, the employee wants permission and leadership in how to resolve it. She believes that punishment for the other side will give her that, but inevitably, even when she sees the other side punished, it does not feel like enough because she has not received the permission and leadership in how to resolve another situation herself. She does not know that she just needs to be taught a few skills and receive permission to use them, and so she will ask for something else and then appear dissatisfied with everything she gets.

That is only because we have been raised to believe that "accountability" and "justice" will make us feel better. Really "accountability" and "justice" are feelings that we create with our beliefs about the circumstances around us. Once we have gone down the path of believing we are victims and that our lives are unjust (even though those beliefs almost always come from very real experiences of victimization and unfairness and seem reasonable), an experience of justice does not shift that belief right away. We have practiced the belief, and so the thought pattern continues even when the external situation is resolved. Responding with effective consequences to someone who is having unacceptable behavior at work is important, but it does not fully address the experience of the person who has practiced self-victimizing beliefs.

When the in-house counsel I talked with said he does not think an employee could be happy under any circumstances, this is the piece he was missing. He has had this experience (most lawyers and business owners have) of seeing an employee try to negotiate a better situation, and even when he receives it remain dissatisfied. We tend to think that the employee is "just a dissatisfied person," but that is actually not a fixed, inalterable class of people. It's not like there are the women, men, non-binary, and dissatisfied. I know you may want to argue with me that I haven't met your mom, but I really know it is true. Dissatisfaction is a skill that we can practice and get very good at, but it is always possible to shift it even in the same job. When I teach Power Dynamics Trainings to employees, I have been impressed to see even extremely dissatisfied, jaded, angry employees engage in making real shifts to create a safe, healthy, productive work environment.

When we go into a reconciliation process expecting employees to fail, we make it easy for them to fail. When we go into it assuming that there are no options, our mind closes down to seeing any options. This doesn't mean there is something wrong with you if that is happening with you – it means you have a human brain. If you are at all concerned that your brain will fall into those traps when you attempt to handle your employees' conflict, give yourself permission to bring someone in who can approach the situation from an unbiased, non-judgmental perspective to give everyone a real chance for reconciliation.

Conclusion

There is so much I want to tell you about how to make your business a wonderful, diverse, inclusive, culturally healthy place! I feel like this book is pretty much too long for a lecture on power dynamics, but not long enough for me to tell you everything I want you to know about the possibilities for resolving and moving forward from crisis conflict in a way that helps your business thrive. I believe this is a skill that everyone can learn, but learning it does not come simply from a logical, competitive negotiation strategy or simply from a contemplative, awareness place. Both are important in order to bring true reconciliation and allow your workplace to have the benefit of an inclusive, transparent environment.

I once worked in a business that did an "investigation" about sexism within the office. One of the business owners, who was also accused of wrongdoing, was the one who conducted the "investigation" because the owners were afraid to have an outside person know about the accusations within the office. A coworker told me that she asked the owner investigating, "Why are you doing this investigation? There needs to be an outside person doing this for you to get good information." The owner responded that they were just not going to do that. As with most investigations, the results came out "inconclusive," because many different people had many different perspectives. As is typical, the person whose report instigated the "investigation" had not wanted an investigation. Within the next year, that office lost at least a quarter of its employees.

Some businesses want to treat high turnover as normal, but in reality it is a huge expense for business owners to train employees to a point of competence (or even worse, to a point of mastery) only to lose them. It is risky to be willing to invest in

ignoring harassment and discrimination to the point of being willing to risk high turnover to allow for those cultural health issues.

It is true that there is a lot of stigma around harassment
and discrimination allegations. Many people believe that if we
acknowledge that our brains have cognitive bias, we will be re-
jected from our communities and face horrible consequences. In
fact, all of our brains have cognitive biases (a.k.a. discrimination).
All of us have been raised with certain privileges and certain disadvantages. Honoring our privileges and questioning our disadvantages is crucial to coming from a place of power and integrity
in every conflict. When a black woman says that a white man is
privileged, it is not an insult, it is a place that the white man has
an opportunity to honor and use in his favor and in the favor of
others who do not have that privilege. Each of us has privileges
that we have the opportunity to honor.

I graduated from law school at a time when the economy
was still struggling and law jobs were hard to find. I went to many
interviews with potential employers who saw Peace Corps on my
resume and were immediately turned off because they did not
believe I could advocate for a tobacco company that was adver-
tising in a way they knew made it more likely to make children
addicted to smoking. They were probably right. Because my
Peace Corps experience was important to my own growth and
advocacy, I decided to keep it on my resume and use it as a test
for potential employers about whether they were willing to be
challenged around making our world a better place. Throughout
those interviews, I was asked over and over again, "What is most
important to you about a workplace?" Every time I answered,
"The people I work with and the environment I work in is the most
important thing." I did not realize at that time how unusual it is to
find a culturally healthy law firm environment. I believe cultures of
secrecy incubate harassment and discrimination.

It is not primarily conservative or liberal, Christian or Muslim, black or white, or male or female, gay or straight workplaces that are facing cultural health infections. It is all of us. The reason is that we have not been taught how to deal with cultural toxicity in the workplace.

When business owners work with me on the preventative side to receive a Workplace Cultural Health Facilitation, I help them with what I believe are the four pillars of cultural wellness in the workplace: Active diagnosis of problems, confidential reporting options, transparency, and a power dynamics facilitation. What I have found is that most businesses that have between twenty-five to seventy-five employees have reached a point of scaling that is too big for the owner to have personal contact with each employee often enough to discover a workplace cultural issue, but not big enough to hire a human resources employee. Beyond that, with businesses that do have human resources departments, many human resources employees have been well trained in the traditional investigation model of response. But, unless they have outside personal training themselves, they have not been taught conflict resolution skills that work in a high-conflict culturally sensitive situation.

There are not many other serious productivity issues that employers are reluctant to acknowledge and invest in. During the Industrial Revolution, we saw something similar, where employers routinely had employees losing limbs and unable to come to work while they healed from being maimed. It was part of their business investment to expect a certain number of employees to be absent from work because of horrific workplace injuries. Many employers now believe that harassment and discrimination is not as serious as physical injuries people experienced during that time, but this is not a belief that serves any of us. When a business is losing employees and losing productivity for *any reason* it seems worth looking at. Whether or not you believe that an employee's subjective pain regarding a harassment, discrimination, or bullying issue is valid is a separate consideration than whether you are losing productivity and losing the investment you have made in your employees.

On the other hand, each of us has experienced the pain of heartbreak, the shame of rejection, the frustration of feeling unheard. That pain, however reasonable or unreasonable, is real and hard to experience. I may think that you are amazing and so I may assume any feeling of rejection, heartbreak, or frustration you have is unrealistic – of course, everyone likes you, I may believe. You may believe the same of me. But, because our suffering is created by our own beliefs, all of our suffering is valid, no matter how painful.

All of our suffering is also optional, even when we don't see that. All of our suffering deserves to be processed, so that we don't become constipated, emotional trash heaps of suffering, but the only way to process suffering that I have found is to acknowledge and have compassion for it. Life is supposed to have both positive and negative. We are supposed to encounter challenges and work through them. That is how we thrive.

In order to create a safe, healthy work environment you need to find out about problems, be open with your business, and respond when you hear about a problem. You don't need to control your employees or create a police state, where no one is allowed to show affection or joke around. Creating an environment where it is safe to talk about the issues that come up, where employees understand they will be respected when they raise a problem, exposes the problems to the sunlight so that they cannot fester.

The first step in this is to do your own work. Understand where you are comfortable addressing these issues yourself and where it is worth having an outside person come in to install the proverbial electrical wiring. No matter how big your cultural conflict at work seems, it is always possible to use it as a starting point for your business's evolution. Your business is worth investing in. Just make sure your investment is not in hiding its wounds, but instead in its growth.

Further Reading

Backlash by Susan Faludi

Awakening Compassion by Pema Chodron

The Gift of Fear by Gavin deBecker

Why Does He Do That? by Lundy Bancroft

Self Coaching 101 by Brooke Castillo

A Mind at Home with Itself by Byron Katie

The Gifts of Imperfection by Brené Brown

Getting to Yes by Roger Fisher and William Ury

The New One Minute Manager by Ken Blanchard

Acknowledgments

It may sound funny to you, but I have struggled with the acknowledgments and my own personal story in writing this book more than any other component of it. At least in part, I think this has been because I genuinely feel grateful for all of the people who have challenged me as much as the people who have nurtured me. How do you narrow down gratefulness for everything that has brought you to where you are now?

Thank you to Angela Lauria and Brooke Castillo who have been examples of business women I know who have created insanely successful businesses by loving and serving people. It is possible for me to do the work I do because of you.

Thank you to the clients who have been willing to share their sorrow and be open to transformation. Each one of you is so incredible! You make my heart bigger every day (but in a good way, not a dangerous-health-condition way). I am not going to name you because of confidentiality, but you know who you are.

Thanks to those of you who have supported my business through your own work and made it possible for my business to grow: Erin Leslie, Alexis Haskett-Wood, Heather Wheeler, and Lou Ter especially. You have been gifts from the universe.

Thank you to the women who have made a spiritual impact in my life: Pema Chodron, Byron Katie, Tamara Arnold, Eliel Fionn, and Tracey Coleman especially.

Thank you to each of you who has sent me an article, tagged me in a post, or commented to me that you saw something that made you think of me! Thank you as always to the wonderful business owners, coaches, and friends who have been there to support me, including Erica Smith, Dr. Sarah Hansen, Mandy Vickers, Caryn Gillen, Meg Weber, Beatrice Grace, Jay McAlpin, Ilisa Rooke-Ley, Suzanne Chanti, and Dave and Raquel Holley. All of you are so important to me.

Thank you to the entire staff of The Author Incubator (Tara Kosowski, Bethany Davis, Rae Guyn, and Cheyenne Giesecke, you know you get special mentions) and all of my co-authors (Mary Tan, my signatory from the universe, and Sandra Bicknell, my sister author, especially) who have been inspiring and caring to say the least.

Thank you to Morgan James for caring, working with me, and making my work so much better than it was when it came to you.

Thank you also to each of the bosses I have worked for who has unreasonably yelled at me or demeaned me. Thank you to the employees I have supervised whom I have found difficult. Thank you to the men who have sexually harassed, threatened, and kidnapped me. Thank you to the abusers I have seen hurt others. These are not sarcastic acknowledgments, but I would not have been able to see what it looks like to successfully resolve high-stress, high-conflict situations without having experienced them myself. As much as seeing successful women ahead of me, seeing abusers has taught me what is possible in terms of trans-formation, growth, and thriving.

Thank you to each reader who is willing to take the time to read this book! You make the world a better place!

About the Author

Meredith Holley is a lawyer, certified life coach, and best-selling author. She helps good business owners create healthy workplace cultures so that they can focus on the important work they have to do in the world. She is the author of *Career Defense 101: How to Stop Sexual Harassment Without Quitting Your Job.*

After law school, Meredith achieved her dream of becoming a civil rights lawyer, advocating for women around sexual assault and harassment issues. The problem was that she was being sexually harassed at the same time. Not wanting to quit her job, Meredith researched and learned everything she could about how to actually stop and prevent sexual harassment, not just for herself, but also for her clients. She went to other lawyers who told her she could file a lawsuit, but if she did not want to do that, "Things are really sexist, and you just have to deal with it." After more than a year of the harassment, she found tools that worked. Her harasser apologized, stopped touching her, and they worked together for years after. She has seen client after client achieve similar results.

Meredith founded Eris Conflict Resolution to help employees and their companies resolve crisis allegations of harassment and discrimination without the costs and stress of turnover and lawsuits.

Meredith lives in Oregon with her angry, elderly, deaf cat, Cressida. She was a Peace Corps volunteer in Ukraine, where she taught English in 2003. Meredith loves peonies, meditation, anything metaphysical, and British zombies.

(Meredith took this photo after sitting for an hour with a woman on New Year's Eve 2018, while the woman sobbed about the abuse she experienced at work. Meredith wanted to share it with you.)

Website: www.ErisResolution.com
Email: Meredith@ErisResolution.com
Facebook: meredith.holley
Instagram: @meredithholley

About Difference Press

Difference Press is the exclusive publishing arm of The Author Incubator, an educational company for entrepreneurs – including life coaches, healers, consultants, and community leaders – looking for a comprehensive solution to get their books written, published, and promoted. Its founder, Dr. Angela Lauria, has been bringing to life the literary ventures of hundreds of authors-in-transformation since 1994.

A boutique-style self-publishing service for clients of The Author Incubator, Difference Press boasts a fair and easy-to-understand profit structure, low-priced author copies, and author-friendly contract terms. Most importantly, all of our #incubatedauthors maintain ownership of their copyright at all times.

Let's Start a Movement with Your Message

In a market where hundreds of thousands of books are published every year and are never heard from again, The Author Incubator is different. Not only do all Difference Press books reach Amazon bestseller status, but all of our authors are actively changing lives and making a difference.

Since launching in 2013, we've served over 500 authors who came to us with an idea for a book and were able to write it and get it self-published in less than 6 months. In addition, more than 100 of those books were picked up by traditional publishers and are now available in book stores. We do this by selecting the

highest quality and highest potential applicants for our future pro-
grams.

Our program doesn't only teach you how to write a book — our team of coaches, developmental editors, copy editors, art directors, and marketing experts incubate you from having a book idea to being a published, bestselling author, ensuring that the book you create can actually make a difference in the world. Then we give you the training you need to use your book to make the difference in the world, or to create a business out of serving your readers.

Are You Ready to Make a Difference?

You've seen other people make a difference with a book. Now it's your turn. If you are ready to stop watching and start taking massive action, go to http://theauthorincubator.com/apply/.

"Yes, I'm ready!"

Other Books by Difference Press

Can You Be a Hypnotist?: How to Create a Fulfilling and Lucrative Career Helping People with Modern and Professional Hypnosis by Erika Flint, BCH, OB

The Holistic Lawyer: Use Your Whole Brain to Work Smarter, Not Harder by Ritu Goswamy, Esq.

Marriage Happiness Is Possible: The Guide to a Purposeful and Passionate Relationship by William Hutcheson

I Love My Job, but It's Killing Me: The Teacher's Guide to Conquering Chronic Stress and Sickness by Lesley Moffat

A Good Day at School: Take Charge of Emotions so Your Child Can Find Happiness by Kat Mulvaney

Love and the Highly Engaged Team: Make a Difference Through Your Leadership by Maria R. Nebres

Why Is Everyone Having a Baby but Me?: The Guide to Healing for Women Who Suffer from Recurrent Miscarriages by Monisha Ramgahan

Don't Tell Me to Relax!: Decrease Anxiety without Lowering Your Standards by Kelly Rompel

If I Am so Talented, Why Can't I Choose What to Do?: The CLEAR WAY to Find Professional Success by Valentina Savelyeva

Trauma and Abuse Healing: A Therapist's Guide to Using Ritual and Ceremony by Heidi Thompson-Henyon

Twice as Good: Leadership and Power for Women of Color by Mary J. Wardell

Thank You

I just think you are fantastic. I may not know you personally, but anyone who has read a book about how to create an inclusive workplace culture is my kind of person. Like I say, working in an environment that is supportive and thriving is palpably different to me than working in an environment that wants to cover up its cultural wounds (and I have worked in both, believe me). I know every workplace culture can get to a thriving place, no matter how dark it is now. Anything you are facing now that feels overwhelming is possible to overcome. I have seen it and I know it.

I can tell that you are passionate about the work you do and about creating a healthy environment for your employees. Do you want to let me know what your business is? I would love to hear what's going on with you and the amazing work you are doing in the world. Feel free to email me at Meredith@ErisResolution.com and just share what your business is and any questions you have from this book.

If you don't have one already, I would love to offer you a copy of the Employee Handbook I share with the business owners who work with me, just as a thank-you for taking the time to read about this topic I care so much about. It is available at https://ErisResolution.com/handbook if you would like to download a copy. Or click here:

Every step you take toward being open about your own experience and listening to others makes the world a better place. Thank you!

CPSIA information can be obtained
at www.ICGtesting.com
Printed in the USA
LVHW051940300920
667544LV00014B/2043